# Traditional Witchcraft for Field and Hedgerow

# Traditional Witchcraft for Field and Hedgerow

Mélusine Draco

Winchester, UK
Washington, USA

First published by Moon Books, 2012
Moon Books is an imprint of John Hunt Publishing Ltd., Laurel House, Station Approach,
Alresford, Hants, SO24 9JH, UK
office1@o-books.net
www.o-books.com

For distributor details and how to order please visit the 'Ordering' section on our website.

Text copyright: Mélusine Draco 2011

ISBN: 978 1 84694 801 5

A CIP catalogue record for this book is available from the British Library.

Design: Stuart Davies


Printed in the UK by CPI Antony Rowe
Printed in the USA by Offset Paperback Mfrs, Inc

We operate a distinctive and ethical publishing philosophy in all
areas of our business, from our global network of authors to
production and worldwide distribution.

# CONTENTS

# Author Biography

Mélusine Draco originally trained in the magical arts of traditional British Old Craft with Bob and Mériém Clay-Egerton. She has been a magical and spiritual instructor for over 20 years with Arcanum and the Temple of Khem, and writer of numerous popular books including *Liber Agyptius: the Book of Egyptian Magic; The Egyptian Book of Days; The Egyptian Book of Nights; The Thelemic Handbook; The Hollow Tree,* an elementary guide to the Qabalah; *A Witch's Treasury of the Countryside; Root & Branch: British Magical Tree Lore* and *Starchild: a rediscovery of stellar wisdom.* Her highly individualistic teaching methods and writing draws on ancient sources, supported by academic texts and current archaeological findings. She now lives in Ireland near the Galtee Mountains.

Her latest titles *Traditional Witchcraft for Urban Living; Traditional Witchcraft for the Seashore; Traditional Witchcraft for Fields and Hedgerows; Traditional Witchcraft for Woods and Forests* and *The Dictionary of Magic & Mystery* are published by O-Books

**Both *Traditional Witchcraft for Fields and Hedgerows* and *Traditional Witchcraft for Woods and Forests* assume a certain degree of magical understanding on the part of the reader with regard to routine divination, spell and Circle casting. For this reason the text does not include the basic elements of rudimentary witchcraft that can be found in titles similar to *Traditional Witchcraft for Urban Living* and *Traditional Witchcraft for the Seashore.***

# Chapter One

# Fields and Hedgerows

*Lost in such ecstasies in this old spot*
*I feel the rapture which the world hath not,*
*That joy like health that flushes in my face*
*Amid the brambles of this ancient place ...*
John Clare

For a witch the magical energies of *Traditional Witchcraft for Fields and Hedgerows* differs quite considerably from *Traditional Witchcraft for Woods and Forests* because whereas the woods have been part of our landscape since the beginning of time, fields and hedgerows are a relatively recent innovation. It therefore stands to reason that the witchcraft of fields and hedgerows is going to be much more of a domestic and homely variety, not moving far from hearth or cattle byre. It will lack the primitive, sometimes hostile, sensations that we encounter when walking alone in the woods. Unfortunately, very few modern witches have the opportunity to understand the land, but once we learn to appreciate it again and begin to feel part of it, it begins to share its secrets.

It's not only woods that can be dated from the variety and number of different species, hedgerows also have their own history and this is chronicled by certain tell-tale signs, familiar to a local witch or cunning woman. Hedgerows are a prominent and distinctive feature of the landscape and the oldest are probably remnants of the continuous woodland that once covered most of the land. As villagers and landowners cleared the forest for agriculture, they would leave the last few feet of forest standing to mark the outer boundaries of their land. A traditional witch will know that these boundaries have a special magical significance, especially at dawn and dusk.

Some of our most ancient hedges are the remnants of such boundaries, perhaps even now still marking parish borders. Hedges were also formed to enclose patches of land to contain livestock. This would have been done close to a farm or village, and in many places, these small, irregular enclosures can still be recognised by witches of today, as indications of old field patterns and ancient hedgerow. The majority, however, were planted in the 18th and 19th centuries to enclose patches of land in order to establish ownership. Nevertheless, the older the hedge, the more we will feel we are walking in our ancestors' footsteps as we search for magical and medicinal ingredients.

For both countrywomen and witches the hedge was extremely important. A veritable treasure house: a source of food, drink, medicine, shelter, fuel and dyes, while numerous superstitions arose around many hedgerow plants. The special plant community that makes up a mature hedgerow also offers a wider range of food for animals and birds than most deciduous woodland, making the hedge a very attractive habitat in winter. After feasting on the autumn harvest of elder and blackberries, birds turn to rosehips and haws, then sloes, and finally to ivy berries and this is where we become familiar with our totem animal or bird in its natural habitat.

The Romans introduced a large number of herbs to Britain, valuing them for their supposed supernatural powers, as well as culinary and medicinal uses ... and many of these plants now grow profusely in the wild. By the Middle Ages, the use of herbs for magical purposes was commonplace, and every village had its own witch or cunning-woman. A medieval witch was an expert in the identification of wild herbs, and from the countryside surrounding her home she would gather the appropriate plants for scenting linen, flavouring sauces ... or procuring an abortion. Herbs were so important in daily life that when people moved around the country, they took with them the plants and the superstitions surrounding them.

Unlike the wort-lore of traditional witchcraft, however, folk or domestic plant medicine was the everyday use of plants by ordinary people to cure minor wounds and ailments. Although there is a wealth of material from the classic herbalists recorded by the Benedictine monk Aelfric, the Physicians of Myddfai and the 17th century apothecary, physician and astrologer, Nicholas Culpeper, very little has actually been preserved of the common *domestic* plant remedies used by our forebears.

In fact, the use of common native plants in everyday home medicine is now almost obsolete, largely because it was mainly a DIY collection of first aid remedies, often passed on orally, rather than a written record. As a result, even many of today's witches are unaware of the therapeutic effects of ordinary kitchen herbs. With proper care and caution, the same herb used to flavour cooking can be used in a more concentrated form to relieve pain. For example:

- Marjoram acts as a circulatory stimulant and helps to relieve circulation problems.
- Parsley can be chewed to help combat bad breath.
- Sage has antiseptic properties and makes an effective gargle for a sore throat.
- Rosemary is a warming circulatory stimulant that can relieve fatigue.
- Thyme has an expectorant action and can be used to relieve chesty coughs.

Simple home remedies did not require any accompanying magical ritual to make them work; a countrywoman would merely pick the necessary plants from the garden or hedgerow to make a preparation for the family's fever, or to treat a wound. For example, a hot infusion made from yarrow, comfrey and cayenne, increased perspiration and helped to reduce a high fever. In fact, towards the end of WWI, the British government used tons of sphagnum moss placed directly on wounds as surgical dressing, when the demand for cotton bandages could not be met. Fortunately, this folk-remedy had not faded from memory — and is still used in some rural areas today.

Similarly, feverfew has been used since the Middle Ages for its analgesic properties. Culpeper recommended the herb for 'all pains in the head', while current research has proven the efficacy of feverfew in the relieving of migraines and headaches when taken as a tea. The common plantain has long been recognised as an excellent restorative and tonic for all forms of respiratory congestions — nasal catarrh, bronchitis, sinusitis and middle ear infections. The plant's demulcent qualities make it useful in an infusion for painful urination. As a lotion, plantain also calms the irritation and itching of insect bites, stings and skin irritations; and as a disinfectant and styptic for wounds ... and how many of us automatically search for a dock leaf after a close encounter with a stinging nettle?

Despite all its magical connotations and Faere connections, the elder tree has long been known as the 'poor man's medicine chest' because its bark, flowers and berries have so many uses in treating respiratory infections and fevers. The leaves make a useful ointment for bruises, sprains and wounds, while an ointment made from the flowers is excellent for chilblains. The inner bark has a history of use as a purgative dating back to the time of Hippocrates ... not forgetting the 'tonic' of elderflower champagne and elderberry wine.

Nevertheless, in *Memory, Wisdom & Healing: The History of Domestic Plant Medicine*, Gabrielle Hatfield makes a valid point about village 'wise women' in that once an individual gained a reputation as a healer, they were immediately set apart from ordinary folk and credited with certain powers. Once this had happened, the healers became increasingly motivated to shroud their practice in mystery and magic, (and this in turn set them still further apart from the rest of the village), expecting some form of payment in kind or money for their services.

In *Traditional Witchcraft for Urban Living*, however, this author observed that although herbs have been grown for many purposes, the gift of healing (herbal or otherwise) is obviously a *natural* one. It might also suggest that many of those who faced the noose accused of witchcraft, were often no more than simple healers with an understanding of potions made from plant extract but with no Craft associations whatsoever. In the meantime, as Dr Harold Selcon records in *The Physicians of Myddfai*, that by the end of the 14th century a different class of medical herbalist was developing — the apothecaries — who purchased herbs collected from the countryside by wandering professional herb collectors, known as the 'green men and women'.

The apothecaries might buy the goods to pass on to their town-dwelling customers, but it was the 'green men and women' who knew *what* to collect and *when*. And this is also an important part of traditional Craft wort-lore. It isn't enough to know that moneywort can be used as a lotion and applied to wounds; or that a teaspoon of dried cowslip flowers taken as a tea will prevent insomnia. It is also necessary to learn *when* to collect them; *how* to prepare and store the plants; *what* to mix with them and in what quantity, before they can be of genuine use.

Gabrielle Hatfield also believes that too much has been made of the link between magic, witchcraft, superstition and plant medicine. She maintains that the image of the herb-gatherer only collecting plants at certain time of the day, and in dark and shady places, has twisted the truth, and turned herb collecting into a dark mysterious ritual. Here we have another case of academic viewpoint unable to accept that *genuine* witches and cunning folk were fully aware that many plant constituents could vary in their concentration, depending on the season, and how, when and where they were gathered. Although many useful plants *were* common knowledge, others were so potent or deadly, that their use and identity was a closely guarded secret. Craft's most esoteric remedies have seldom been revealed to *cowans* (i.e. outsiders), while the sceptical learn nothing at all.

Nevertheless, prior to, and during the First and Second World Wars, Britain grew large quantities of its own medicinal herbs; while a significant quantity of wild herbs were gathered for commercial use. The 'wild herb men' finally went out of business in the early 1960s, although in December 1972, the *East Anglian Magazine* featured an article on one of the last men to gather wild plants for a living. This occupation was a traditional one with a long history, and during the reign of Elizabeth I the 'Wild Herb Act' was passed, giving the 'green-men' the right to gather herbs and roots in wild uncultivated land.

Through the daily life of ordinary country people, however, the use of folk medicine had been preserved with remarkable accuracy from one generation to another up until the early 20th century. As a result of two world wars and with the large-scale dispersal of country people into the towns, the need for folk-medicine diminished outside the practice of traditional witch-craft. Old people who remained, no longer had anyone left to whom they could pass this age-old wisdom and so much of it died out for lack of interest. In many cases, only the remedy surviving to pass into folklore and superstition. For the tradi-tional witch, however, wort-lore is part of her (or his) heritage and must be preserved by developing a greater understanding of the fields and hedgerows where these plants can still be found.

It doesn't matter whether we refer to ourselves as witch, wiccan, or pagan. Whether we belong to a coven, or consider ourselves to be a solitary but important part of the larger pagan community ... when we observe what we can view as 'field Craft', more often than not, we tend to work alone. The benefits of being a solitary witch means we can work whenever we feel like it, regardless of the date on the calendar, the phase of the moon, or what anyone else considers to be a 'right' or 'wrong' time of the day. The only 'rule' we need to learn and obey, is the call of the natural cyclic tides of Nature ... nothing else.

And whether we live in the country, town or city, Nature *is* all around us. It cannot be suppressed, destroyed or eradicated and if Nature suddenly ceased to be, then every living thing on the planet would die. No book ever written can teach us how to become a witch. Only Nature can do that. Only Nature can coax out those long suppressed abilities and give us back the freedom to be a witch, releasing the knowledge of the Old Ways back into the world. So let's walk through the fields and along the hedgerow together and discover Nature as she moves through the year ...

Warning: For hundreds of years the hedgerows have provided witches with all the ingredients for their healing potions. It is unwise, however, to guess as to the identities of those with which you are unfamiliar. Many plants, such as the *Umbelliferae* family, can look very similar but may contain one kind that is poisonous — e.g. hemlock! The most common problems in herbal treatment are not the side effects but the reactions to misguided self-diagnosis; the wrong herb may compound the problem.

## Visualisation Exercise

Not all witches will have access to open fields and hedgerows. Some of us may never move out of the towns or cities — and many more will not be familiar with British flora and fauna because they live in other parts of the world. Nevertheless, our country-born ancestors, when they moved further afield, took their knowledge and beliefs with them — and learned to improvise. And along with their own traditions, they would probably have absorbed some of the knowledge of local peoples — from the native Americans to the Australian aboriginals — in order to utilise the magical energies of the flora and fauna of their new country.

Nevertheless, everyone — regardless of where they live — will be able to picture in their mind's eye, the summer lushness of an English buttercup meadow ... even if they have never set foot in the British Isles. We may need to use picture books to aid visualisation to begin with, but it isn't difficult to look *into* a picture or photograph and visualise ourselves actually viewing that scene. We only have to stretch out our hand and pick the flowers ...

**Try this simple exercise:**
Pick a common wild flower, possibly one that is considered to be a weed, **from a piece of waste ground or local building site** and identify it; remembering that many so-called weeds have medicinal or magical properties. Discover all you can about it and press the flower between the pages of your magical journal, recording the notes as you find out more about the plant. The power of the witch is a natural ability and with practice, we should be able to visualise the flower in its *natural wild environment*, not the place where it was found.

For example, we have discovered a small clump of Herb Robert growing amongst the rubble on a new supermarket site. This distinctive little pink flower with its colourful fern-like leaves is recommended by Culpeper for: 'It speedily heals wounds and is effectual in old ulcers in the privy parts or elsewhere ...' Its modern usage, is listed in the *RHS Encyclopaedia of Herbs and Their Uses* as being suitable for use internally for gastro-intestinal infections and externally for treating skin eruptions. Now visualise the flower in its *natural* setting, growing at the foot of a hedgebank with the summer breeze causing the delicate leaves to flutter; there is someone in period costume — perhaps one of the 'green' men or women gathering plants to sell to the apothecaries in London — bending to pick the plant ...

Once you have proved to yourself that you can immediately visualise the pictures painted in the text of *Traditional Witchcraft for Fields and Hedgerows,* you can create your own fields and hedgerows on the astral. And walk there whenever you please.

## To make a Hawthorn Witch Ball

*On New Year's Day the women of the house should cut a selection of long, thin branches of hawthorn and plait them into a sphere. This should be dried in the oven/hearth and suspended in the kitchen until the following New Year. While the women of the household were making a new ball, the men would take the old hawthorn ball out into the fields and set light to it. According to tradition, it should be carried so that pieces of the burning hawthorn fall into the furrows in order to bring life and fertility to the crops.* For a special charm to bring good fortune into your home, burn the ball in the garden and when it has been rendered down to ash, sprinkle the remains around the boundary of your property for good luck.

Chapter Two

# January — Dead Moon

January is the Dead Moon — the time of the year when snow usually makes its appearance and from the Old Celtic for 'the end of winter' in a calendar where February was the first month of spring. Represented by the Rowan, otherwise known as mountain ash, sprigs of this tree are considered to bring good luck, and to protect from negative magic and the evil eye. An old Celtic salutation was: 'Peace be here and rowan tree!' Twelfth Night falls on the 6th January, when many Old Craft witches celebrate the old Midwinter Festival according to the Julian calendar. The Anglo-Saxons called it *Wolfmonath*, when wolves moved closer to human habitation to feed off the carcases of fallen stock. The 14th century misericord country calendar shows it as the time for collecting firewood.

With modern climate change knocking the seasons out of kilter, there is something re-assuring about deep snow and freezing conditions around Midwinter and the New Year. We may be inconvenienced for a few days by electricity cuts and frozen pipes, but for a brief moment, we have an insight into how our ancestors viewed these conditions: huddling together for warmth around a meagre fire, with fuel and food supplies running low, and wolves prowling outside, waiting to feed off the dead. Snow represents tradition, custom and history — **the ancestral life-blood of traditional British witchcraft.**

But with the thaw will come flooding, turning vast tracts of river valleys into monumental lakes — recalling the time when much of our lowlands were covered by sea. This is a mysterious frozen world where trees loom ghost-like out of the mist.

Everything is covered with a glittering film of hoare-frost that forms when moisture in the air freezes on cold surfaces (usually overnight), producing ice crystals in the shape of scales, needles, feathers and fans. This heavy frost represents magic, mystery and Otherworld — **the spiritual life-blood of traditional British witchcraft.**

There is an old country saying that a foot of snow is worth an inch of rain, simply because melting snow slowly percolates down into the subsoil. For all the disruption it causes, the thawing process is so slow that most of the water finds its way into the underground water systems, the maze of streams flowing along the underworld of the land. Our winter weather is Nature's way of demonstrating that, despite all the scientific discoveries, humans have little control over life on the planet. With this rather stark reminder that all was not rosy in the countryside of our ancestors, it is the ideal time to start to familiarise ourselves with the bare bones of Nature and begin to identify the flora and fauna that appear on the blank canvas of the year.

January is the month when all seems to be stillness and silence. Small animals remain hidden, hibernating, or sleeping to conserve energy. Migrant birds left in the autumn and it will be many months before they return. Insects are dead or dormant. The fields seem empty but even in these freezing conditions, the delicate green shoots of the woodbine, or wild honeysuckle, can be detected in the hedgerow. The weak winter sun reflects on the bright yellow flowers of a sheltered gorse bush, even if the blossoms are seared by frost.

The banks of the hedgerow house the rabbit warrens but the entrances often look undisturbed because while the snow lies on the ground, only a few rabbits venture out to travel a few yards down the hedge and disappear again. By the end of the month, they will be out in greater numbers to find what nourishment they can from the young grass. Their droppings are everywhere but never more than a couple of yards from the shelter of the hedge.

Foxes too, are active, for here and there are signs of disturbed earth at the entrance to the larger burrows, and a few feet from the hedge are the unidentifiable remains of what was once a small, furry animal. Yet another reminder for the traditional witch that Nature, although beautiful and mysterious, is also red in tooth and claw. In *The Country Book of the Year*, Dennis Furnell writes that the snow 'is as useful a clue as is the murder weapon to the detective'. Here we find the telltale signs of scurrying mice in the hedge-bottom; the paired 'snowshoe' imprints of rabbits at the field margin, or the purposeful straight line of fox-tracks that chronicle the previous night's hunting.

The snow also records the strongly scented territory markings the dog-fox leaves as his calling card. January is the month when foxes mate, with the vixen's shrill, yelping scream echoing eerily in the darkness, answered by the sharp, staccato bark of the dog fox. **The traditional witch knows that at the conclusion of a magical working, the answering call of a fox (or dog) is the sign that the spell has gone home.**

January, of course, is named after Janus, the Roman two-faced god of vigil and doorways, who looked backwards to the old year, and forward to the new one. Even as late as the early 1900s, the old Roman custom of *strena* was still being observed in rural parts of Glamorgan, Carmarthen and Monmouth. Small boys would collect the *calenning* (New Year gifts of pennies and small cakes) although the practice of decorating oranges and apples had largely died out. The fruit was pierced with corn, holly and mistletoe and stuck with three skewers to serve as a stand when not being held. A fourth skewer acted as a handle. The *strena* was a Roman symbol of fruitfulness for the coming year.

Wrenning, or 'hunting the wren' is another of those old customs that survived from ancient times right up until the 20th century. The wren is a winter singer whose song is very loud for such a tiny bird; it is a clear, jubilant trill. This busy little bird with its characteristic erect tail, scurries around in the undergrowth or flies for short distances close to the ground. Although usually unsociable and aggressive, in winter the wren will roost communally for warmth in some small cavity. Despite its diminutive size, wrens are fearless birds that will mob predators, such as owls, cats or stoats with a loud rattling alarm call.

Probably this bravery led the wren to represent the spirit of the old year doing battle with the robin, representing the spirit of the new. Believed to be an enactment of the old regeneration theme (the Old King being sacrificed to make way for the Young King) the wren and the robin were probably chosen because these birds are the boldest, and most likely to risk coming close to humans during cold, lean times.

Although the wren has always enjoyed a certain protection as a sacred bird, on one day of the year it was hunted and killed. As an example of transference magic, the wren was expected to shoulder all the ills and problems of the people; effectively taking their bad luck, ill health, and so forth leaving them free to hope for good health and prosperity in the coming year. Traditionally, the tree of the wren is the ivy, while the robin is allocated the holly. A simple rite that could be performed instead of the actual killing of a wren could be as follows:

A traditional substitute for a wren was a ball of sheep wool collected from the hedgerow and dyed brown. In the late afternoon before the Winter Solstice, visit your local hedgerow and ritually cut a length of flowering ivy, stating as you do so, that you are honouring the spirit of the Old Year. Wrap the ivy in a piece of silk and carry it home. Place the ivy in a central part of the house, where it can absorb all the dross accrued over the year — perhaps as part of the festive decorations.

At dawn of Twelfth Night, re-wrap the ivy in its silk and, together with the wool, return to the hedge. Locate a strong *male* holly tree and wind the ivy and wool round the base of the trunk, stating your intention.

Offer thanks to the spirit of the ivy/wren and then leave the ivy to die.

The intention of this ritual is to offer the life force of the old year in sacrifice, to the spirit of the new, so that it can flourish with extra vigour (as will your own fortune). Light a small fire and burn the silk (silk headscarves can be obtained quite cheaply from most charity shops). This represents the destroying aspect of the Goddess and by performing this rite, you will have enacted the entire birth-death-regenerative cycle. The reason why the traditional Midwinter 'hunting of the wren' now takes place in early January is because the shift from the Julian to the Gregorian calendar in 1582 meant 11 days were lost in the process.

Although robins have endeared themselves to countless generations, they are also extremely aggressive and territorial. In fact, the robin or 'ruddock', size for size would out-gun an eagle in terms of ferociousness. Both the robin and the wren would be excellent totems for a witch, and an amulet of a wren can be carried in the form of an old British farthing coin (if necessary, purchased off eBay) that has a wren featured on its reverse.

While others will be taking down the festive decorations, the 6th January marks Twelfth Night when, as we have seen, many traditional witches celebrate Old Midwinter according to the Julian calendar. The clever witch will have a wide circle of pagan friends that will allow them to party from Saturnalia on the 17th December right through to Twelfth Night on 6th January! Twelfth Night customs are many and varied across the country, being another relic of the Roman festivities ... such as drawing lots with beans to see who would be King and Queen of Misrule for the duration.

After the introduction of the Gregorian calendar, Twelfth Night was often celebrated with far more feasting and merry-making than Christmas, which was then observed as a religious festival. The church also attempted to align it with Epiphany (the period when the star appeared to the wise men of the East) but never managed to get rid of the pagan overtones. Although the practice was eventually prohibited in 1555, the Lord of Misrule presided over the entire festival as a 'master of mirth and fun' having been appointed on All-Hallows Eve (31st October) until Candlemas (2nd February). This ancient symbolism can be found in the Sacrificial King traditions where a substitute king is feted and then sacrificed to ensure the prosperity of the people. An ideal celebration for Twelfth Night would be a fancy dress party, particularly one that involved some form of cross-dressing, when the Lord and Lady of Misrule entertain their guests.

Ploughing the fields in preparation for sowing was the first task of the agricultural year and the first Monday after Twelfth Night is still known as Plough Monday. This was the day on which farmhands returned to work after the Midwinter holiday — not that any work was actually done as the day was marked by various customs and merrymaking, with mumming plays and a 'Molly dance'.

Out in the fields, however, the traditional witch heralds each season as it comes, marking the changes with quiet observance and celebration. She or he will know that those old-fashioned, bleak January days are becoming a thing of the past since weather patterns have changed drastically over the last three centuries. The month is now warmer, wetter and sunnier, and less snowy than at any other time since the start of weather recording. *Then*, January was consistently cold, bringing with it dry, freezing conditions; snowfalls were more frequent and lay much longer during the colder months.

The present climate means that a warm January tends to be much wetter but the witch takes advantage of those rare, frosty days to wander the fields and lanes in the early mornings before the winter sun melts the frost ...

... to experience those first magical moments when the winter sun breaks over the skyline to spread its scarlet fingers across the white, frozen landscape,

... or to watch the sun go down in a blaze of fire over the tree tops.

A traditional witch will be out and about at dawn and dusk to utilise the magical energies of this 'time between times', especially at the boundaries and borders of the field margin. It may not be conducive for elaborate outdoor ritual but there is still a great deal of magical energy to be drawn from the landscape. If the weather is mild enough, the witch will know where to find the first flowering of celandines, anemones and primroses, and watch for the signs of the trees awakening from their deep, winter sleep.

Although not native to Britain, the rabbit is now one of the most familiar of wild animals. Usually they only emerge at dawn and dusk, but during the winter months, they can be seen searching for food at any time. Gnawed bark on a beech tree is a sign that rabbits are hungry. When they appear from their burrows to feed much earlier than usual, it tells us they are preparing for an enforced food shortage due to stormy weather approaching. Similar behaviour by rooks and other birds, and animals also heralds the approach of bad weather. A rabbit's foot is reputed to bring good luck to anyone who carries it as a talisman and a luck-bringing custom still widely practised is to say 'Rabbits!' on the first day of every month. The charm should be said aloud three times early in the morning before any other word is spoken.

Bearing all this in mind, the witch is well advised to bond with a totem animal that is native to the landscape. It is all very well choosing an exotic creature from another culture but this restricts contact to astral working, whereas an animal that is part of the surrounding fields can always be encountered on the *physical* plane. For example, a witch moving from Wales, where she daily encountered the call of the buzzard and red kite, could wait a *long* time for either of these raptors to present itself in Ireland. For magical purposes, the kestrel is ideal substitute and, although not as spectacular as the Welsh birds, it is still a raptor, and does have a certain grace of its own.

The bare, winter landscape is a perfect backdrop for observing the antics of the sparrowhawk and the change in the behaviour of starlings tells us when there's a hawk about. The birds take no notice of a kestrel but if a sparrowhawk makes an appearance, the flock has been known to head for the nearest sheep field and drop down among the grazing animals. They will remain on the ground among the legs of the sheep until the sparrowhawk glides away. There is also a lot of confusion between the sparrowhawk and kestrel. The kestrel hunts by hovering over a roadside verge — something a sparrowhawk would not do. The sparrowhawk is a woodland bird and except for the late winter and early spring when it can be seen circling, and often encountered sweeping low over hedgerows and along country lanes.

The traditional witch develops an affinity with Nature that she recognises as being part of her own personal universe. Whenever she (or he) walks in the fields and along the hedgerow, there are signs and messages that are communicated to her on many different levels. Which is why it is much more 'convenient' to have a totem animal that can be encountered during the normal course of a day's ramble. On a day-to-day basis, the witch interacts with Nature and learns to read the signs of the hidden world that exists only feet away from unsuspecting eyes.

## The Hearth Fire

The hearth fire is the symbolic and magical centre of any witch's home, and it is to the hearth we bring the richness of Nature's bounty to help celebrate the old festivals and feast days. It is at the hearth fire we regularly use the four sacramental foods that have been part of spiritual observance since ancient times, oil (Elemental Fire), bread (Elemental Air), salt (Elemental Earth) and wine (Elemental Water).

Just into the New Year on the 5th January is Wassail Eve when apple trees were offered libations of cider to encourage fruitfulness in the orchards during the coming year, and pieces of bread soaked in cider were placed in the crooks of the trees. Guns were fired to frighten away any evil spirits — but in the post-gun law days, it can be just as effective to use Chinese crackers.

## Wassail!

*Wassail* is the old salutation uttered when drinking a person's health, and also refers to the liquor in which such healths were drunk, especially ale with roasted apples, sugar and nutmeg. This simple recipe was traditionally prepared to toast the apple trees on 5th January (or on Twelfth Night) to ensure a bumper harvest in the coming year.

## Wassail

*6 cooking apples*
*Soft brown sugar*
*½ oz ground ginger*
*½ grated nutmeg*
*pinch of powdered cinnamon*
*8 oz Demerara sugar*
*3 pints mild or brown ale*
*½ bottle of raisin wine*
*¼ bottle of sherry*
*1 lemon*
*lump sugar*

Core the apples but do not peel them. Fill the holes with soft brown sugar and roast in a moderate oven for 45 minutes to 1 hour. Take care they do not burst. Mix in a saucepan the ginger, nutmeg, cinnamon and Demerara sugar. Add 1 pint of the ale and bring to the boil. Stir in the rest of the ale, the wine and 10 lumps of sugar that have been rubbed on the rind of the lemon. Heat the mixture but do not allow it to boil this time. Put the roasted apples in a large punch bowl and pour in the hot ale mixture with half the peeled and sliced lemon.

The plentiful supply of wild pigeon and pheasant at this time of the year means that game still plays an important part in rural kitchens; roast pheasant and pigeon breasts make a pleasant change to normal fare. The pheasant has always been highly prized for the table ... 'Eaten at precisely the right moment, its flesh is tender, sublime and highly flavoured, for it has at once something of the flavour of poultry and of venison.' (Brillat-Savarin 19th century)

### Recipe for Pheasant Breasts

Coat pheasant breasts with egg and breadcrumbs. Lay them flat in a buttered sauté pan. Add a few drops of lemon juice; cover the sauté pan and cook for 6 to 8 minutes in a very hot oven. Cooking must be extremely rapid and done without boiling. The liquid must be limited to the few drops of lemon juice. Place on a warm dish and garnish with a green vegetables tossed in butter.

In the cold month of January there is little available by way of 'wild food' during the Dead Moon. If the frost hasn't been too severe, we may be lucky enough to find a supply of chickweed in the garden or field edge. This common weed can be cooked with spring onions as a fresh vegetable, or served as a salad, according to Richard Mabey's *Food For Free*. It has also been used as a healing plant for centuries and listed by Culpeper for relieving itching skin conditions.

## Weatherwise

January is usually the coldest month of the year and there's a country saying that *as the days lengthen, the cold strengthens.* For those who pay attention to weather lore, frost and snow are not unwelcome sights at this time — in fact, mild weather during any of the winter months (especially January) is a bad omen:

- *Summer in winter, and a summer's flood, never boded England good.*
- *If January calends be summerly gay, 'twill be winterty weather till the calends of May.*
- *A January spring is good for nothing.*

Although the shortest day is past, January is a dark month in northern Europe; the nights are still long, and in dull weather, it often feels as if there is little daylight at all. Frost, ice and snow take their toll on non-hibernating wildlife, particularly birds. A witch would pay close attention to the weather in order to impress her neighbours, and to make provision for her own activities.

## The Turning of the Year

Here we take two views of the rhythm of the seasons. One is the series of carved choir seats in St Mary's Church, Ripple, showing a remarkable roundup of country life dating back 600 years to the 14th century, giving a glimpse of a country calendar with religious overtones. Life was harder then, but the essentials of the farming year were much the same as they are now. The modern version is taken from a series of photographs seen from the same spot in the Buckinghamshire countryside, showing the ever-changing pattern of the fields throughout the year.

**Then:** Collecting dead boughs for the hearth fire.

**Now:** Beyond the hedge, the winter wheat is springing up.

**The Circle ritual for the month should reflect the celebration of new beginnings.** Collect firewood or kindling as a symbolic gesture and make a supply of miniature faggots (bundles) for burning during magical workings. Ideally, these should be made from any of the Nine Sacred Woods, ash, birch, yew, hazel, rowan, willow, pine, thorn, or other indigenous trees recognised as being traditionally sacred, with the exception of oak or elder. The faint bloom of the winter wheat is a sign of new beginnings and although we are still in the Dead Moon, there is the symbol of hope springing eternal.

### Rowan Magic

The rowan, or mountain ash, is a particularly magical tree — even the Christians adopted its use as a preventative charm against witches! Tie a red ribbon to a berry-bearing branch for general good luck and to keep evil and harm at bay, or make your special wish while you do so. Rowan is also one of the trees believed to take away illness. Take a lock of hair from the sufferer and make a slit in the bark of the tree; push the hair into the slit and as the slit heals, so will the patient. The Saxons made use of this healing property by using a special spoon fashioned from rowan wood to stir medicinal potions.

This is a very special wood with many magical properties, perhaps that is why it is particularly useful for psychic protection as it can be utilised in so many different ways; perhaps the best-known traditional spell being the making of a rowan cross. Take two twigs and tie them together with red thread as you chant:

> *Black luggie, Hammer Head,*
> *Rowan tree and Red Thread*
> *Put all evil to its speed.*

In the old days, these crosses were often to be found adorning cattle and horses to prevent them being abducted, or ridden by the Faere Folk — the crosses would also be hung in stables and byres for the same purpose. Cattle herders would cut their droving stick from rowan wood in the belief that this would help fatten their animals.

Locate a number of rowan trees in the vicinity and make a mental note to add rowan jelly to your larder for next winter. The berries first appear in August but are best picked in October by cutting whole clusters from the tree.

### Apple & Rowanberry Jelly

*3 lb rowanberries*
*3 lb apples*
*3 pints water*
*Sugar*

Remove rowanberry stalks, wash and drain the berries. Wash and slice the apples and cook them with the rowanberries and water till soft and broken up. Strain the juice through a scalded jelly bag. Return the juice to the pan, heat and add 1 lb sugar to each pint of juice. Stir till dissolved. Boil rapidly until setting point is reached. Pour into warmed jars and allow to cool before sealing. Use as part of your celebratory offerings around the next Midwinter and Twelfth Night.

## A Witch's Candle Divination

*If a spark flies off the candle it is a sure sign of a letter in the morning. A spark on the wick means a letter for the one who first sees it, and a big glow like a parcel means money coming to you.* A spark on the altar candle indicates that a message will shortly be received, the bigger the spark the more important the message. If the flame begins to burn blue it means that there is a 'spirit' present that can (or should be) be consulted about future events.

Chapter Three

# February — Short Moon

February is the Short Moon. The long, cold days of winter continued to take their toll in times past and some Celtic names allude to the month being cut short — represented by the Ash. 'Fill-dyke' is a term applied to this this month by the East Anglian fenmen recorded in the legends of Hereward the Wake. In old Norse mythology, the World-Tree was an ash, Yggdrasil, the Cosmic Axis. The original Anglo-Saxon name for the month was 'Sprout-kale' for the vegetable that began to sprout at this time. It was also referred to as *Solmonath* or 'cake month' because cakes and other offerings were presented to the gods. In the 14th century misericord calendar, it was shown as the time for hedging and ditching.

During the 5th century the pagan festival of Imbolc (2nd February — to celebrate the start of the Celtic lambing season) was changed to Candlemas — the feast of the Purification, although the name of February comes from an old Roman festival *Februa*. For pagan folk, it is the feast day of Bride or Brigit, the goddess of the British tribe, the Brigantia. Tie a ribbon to the outside of your window to let her know she is welcome in your house.

This authentic 17th century poem by Robert Herrick gives us a glimpse into the customs of the Restoration, which probably have their origins in earlier times.

## Ceremonies for Candlemas Eve

*Down with rosemary and bays*
*Down with the mistletoe;*
*Instead of holly, now upraise*
*The greener box, for show*

*The holly hither did sway;*
*Let box now domineer*
*Until the dancing Easter Day*
*Or Easter's eve appear*

*Then youthful box, which now hath grace*
*Your houses to renew,*
*Grown old, surrender must his place*
*Unto the crisped yew.*

*When yew is out, the birch comes in,*
*And many flowers beside,*
*Both of a fresh and fragrant kin,*
*To honour Whitsuntide.*

*Green rushes then, and sweetest bents,*
*With cooler oaken boughs,*
*Come in for comely ornaments,*
*To re-adorn the house.*
*Thus times do shift, each thing his turn does hold;*
*New things succeed as former things grow old.*

February is a time when all of Nature still appears to be in a state of limbo, halfway between the snows of winter and the warm rain of spring. It is the time for spectacular sunrises and sunsets for which the witch has an in-built appreciation. For those who take the time to stand and stare, there are those few fleeting moments of a true Turneresque skyscape, when a whole kaleido-scope of colour is visible. Turner was often accused of exagger-ating the colours and forms of nature, but as he was alleged to have retorted to the woman who complained that *she* never saw his skies in nature — 'Then God help you, Madam.'

Frogs are coming out of hibernation to find a mate, having been lying in torpor for the coldest months in the mud at the bottom of the pool. From this point, they begin their journey back to the pond where they hatched in a previous spring. The frog gets its name from the Anglo-Saxon word *frogga* and is often still referred to by its country name of 'paddock' — the same as for its cousin the toad or *tadde* in Old English. Much frog and toad lore is synonymous with witchcraft and superstition, with both creatures being the victim of cruel mutilation; tadpoles were once swallowed alive in the belief that they cured gout! Conversely, it was widely believed to be unlucky to kill a frog as they were said to possess the soul of a boy or girl who died in childhood.

Toads have a mixed reputation in folklore: they are lucky and more often, unlucky; they can be used in healing charms or as a poison. It is considered lucky to meet a toad – but unlucky to kill one. A toad is capable of eating hundreds of insect at one meal and in times past, was often kept as a household pet and used to clean up cottage pantries infested with ants. They emerge at dusk and often hibernate in disused animal burrows, although they can be encouraged to remain in the garden by providing a suitable spot, so that they deal with snails, slugs, caterpillars and woodlice. **For the traditional witch the croak of a frog or toad at the culmination of a magical working is a sign of its success.**

Early celandines bloom in the south-facing hedgerows, the yellow flowers competing with the scattered pockets of gorse that gallantly flowers throughout the year even if there is only a single spray of flowers. Thus proving the old saying: 'When the gorse is out of bloom, kissing's out of season.'

Early ploughing will bring the seagulls although it's suspected that many of these birds hardly ever see the sea. The name for the gull comes from the old Welsh *gwylan* or Brythonic tongue meaning 'wailing bird' because of its mournful cry and in folklore they were believed to be the souls of fishermen and sailors lost at sea. The birds have been called 'gulls' since the 15th century — a word also meaning 'wailer' in medieval Cornish — the name spread widely during the Tudor period when Cornishmen provided much of the manpower of the English navy. In country weather-lore:

*Seagull, seagull, sit on the sand*
*It's never fine weather when you're on the land*

Fairs were held all over the country from the 13th century and were the life's blood of rural people since it meant they had the opportunity to sell their cattle and goods for a good price. The extra money enabled them to buy essentials that couldn't be acquired by bartering with their neighbours. Generally, these were large markets held on a saint's day where people came to trade as well as enjoy themselves. Each individual fair, which took place at all times of the year except during deep winter, had its own district and in many places, the people could only sell their animals and produce there. A large number took place in November before the onset of winter, allowing people to dispose of unwanted livestock and goods; others were hiring fairs (known as 'mop fairs') where men and women servants were hired. In 1277, King John granted the Bedfordshire town of Biggleswade the right to hold an annual horse fair on 14th February. Many of the older residents can still remember these St Valentine's Day fairs before their ultimate demise in the 1950s.

Unfortunately, the majority of these old country fairs no longer exist but the traditional fare for celebratory dinners was the goose, and English rural history is littered with references to 'Goose Fairs'. The bird has always played an important part in rural life, not only for its meat but because the feathers were used to make down pillows, bed coverings and feather beds — not forgetting that the arrow flights for the English long-bow were grey goose feathers. The large wing-pinion was used for sweeping the hearth and smaller feathers brushed flour and oatmeal from the bake stone.

February, however, is the time for love and romance with (14th) Valentine's Day, (15th) *Lupercalia*, the Feast of Wolves in ancient Rome, a festival of love and fertility, and (29th) Leap Year Day when traditionally women are allowed to propose marriage to their men. Many old country superstitions, particularly those relating to healing, love and romance, have preserved a consider-able amount of Craft-lore in the guise of love charms. Throughout history, girls everywhere have wanted to know whom they would marry and there has been a great deal of witchcraft recorded in Victorian folklore compilations, concealed as harmless love charms.

For example, the folklorist will tell us to collect nine ash keys at midnight and tie them with white thread to place under our pillow to dream of a future husband. The old cunning-woman would have known that the binding of the ash keys could also be used for attracting wealth or information. Nevertheless, as February is traditionally the month of romance, we can gain knowledge of our future partner by plucking those nine ash keys as we chant:

*Even ash, even ash, I pluck thee*
*This night my own true love to see*
*Neither in his/her rick not in his/her rare*
*But in the clothes s/he doth each day wear.*

The keys should then be placed beneath our pillow. Our future spouse will be dressed neither in their 'rick' (rich or best clothes), nor will they be naked ('rare') and we will be able to assess their financial situation, and even the kind of work they do. If we do not have a lover at present, carrying the ash keys in a small fabric bag will help to attract a suitable partner.

During the winter, ash trees are easily recognised by the sooty-black buds arranged in opposite pairs along the twigs. The ash is the last of the trees to show its foliage and the first to lose it in the autumn. Ash wood is both supple and closely grained, resisting shock without splintering and was often used in weaponry. In Norse mythology the *ask* held an honoured place, appearing as Askr, the Father of Mankind. The myth claims that when the gods wanted to populate the earth they took an ash tree and breathed the human soul into it and Askr was born while woman was fashioned from an alder tree. The ash is one of the nine sacred woods and one of the nine Celtic Chieftain Trees.

## The Hearth Fire

In the early morning light we can often find the 'slot marks', or hoof prints of deer in the frozen mud on the farm track. It is hard to imagine that there is a deer problem when we never see them but, as any stalker will tell you, 99 per cent of the human population permanently live within a mile of one type of deer or another. Unfortunately, when deer overpopulate, disease soon kicks in and the death rate from parasites and pneumonia goes up, which is why it is important to keep the numbers at a manageable level. For the generations who have shed a tear over the death of Bambi's mother, the necessity for killing these beautiful creatures is a bitter pill to swallow, but venison made a pleasant change to the meagre winter fare, and one the traditional witch would have looked forward to with relish.

## Roast Venison

Venison is classified as game and the prime cuts are leg and loin, which are usually roasted after it has been marinated. Venison is rarely dry-roasted but braised, the liquid helping to moisten the meat during cooking. The meat should be placed in a roasting tin with a mixture of fat, oil and the wine in which it was marinated; it may also be covered with slices of streaky bacon. The meat is best roasted in an oven preheated to very hot Gas Mark 8/450F/230C and should be basted every 20 minutes with the juices in the tin.

The traditional accompaniment to roast venison is a tart fruit sauce, made with such fruits as redcurrants or cranberries, together with thin gravy and vegetables. A small portion of venison would be an ideal offering for the Old Ones at this time of the year.

Try this 17th century recipe from Yorkshire to accompany venison or venison steaks.

## Old Currant Sauce
*2 oz currants*
*8 fl oz port*
*½ teaspoon ground cloves*
*2 slices bread (crusts removed and made into breadcrumbs)*
*2 oz butter.*

Soak the currants in the port for about an hour, then transfer fruit with the cloves added into a saucepan. Add the breadcrumbs and butter and simmer gently for about 20 minutes until the mixture thickens.

The young shoots of wild food are beginning to emerge and in addition to chickweed there is jack-by-the-hedge on hedgebanks and open woods, and new growth on the nettles. Jack-by-the-hedge has a mild garlicy taste and its chopped leaves can added to salads and sauces. Medicinally it was taken for bronchitis and asthma and applied externally for minor injuries and slow healing skin problems.

**Weatherwise**

February is renowned for having the most unpleasant weather of the year, although farmers welcome the rain and snow because it prepares the ground for sowing and germination of the seed.

- *If in February there be no rain, 'tis neither good for hay nor grain;*
- *Much February snow a fine summer doth show*
- *All months of the year curse a fait February*

A weather prophecy associated with this date claims: *If Candlemas be fair and bright, winter will have another flight; but if Candlemas brings cloud and rain, winter is gone and won't come again.*

In country-lore, it is possible to predict whether we can expect a dry or wet summer by observing: *If the oak before the ash, we will only have a splash. If the ash before the oak, we will have a soak*

The 12th, 13th and 14th days of February were said to have been 'borrowed' from January. If these days proved to be stormy, the year would be favoured with good weather; but if fine, the year would be foul and unfavourable. If the 'horns' of the moon seem to point slightly upwards then the next 28-day cycle will be fine; while if they turn down the period will be wet. Rain can also be expected when a faint outline of the full moon can be seen between the horns of the new moon. A witch would know that if there is a halo around the moon then a snap of cold weather or frost is expected.

**The Turning of the Year**

February is the shortest month of the year — and a good thing too, in view of its weather and the lack of any distinguishing features. On the plus side, it does give some tantalising glimpses of the approach of spring, with the gradual lengthening of the daylight hours, and the first signs of new growth in the hedgerows.

> **Then:** During the short days, hedging and ditching were carried out.
> **Now:** Spring barley is sown in the nearby field. Mild winters bring forward sowing, and bad summers delay harvesting.

**The Circle ritual for the Short Moon should be one of protecting our personal boundaries and magical regeneration, using a bundle of ash twigs.** Since Bride is the ancestral guardian of the sacred flame, candles should be lit and placed in windows as part of the protection rite.

## Ash Magic

From very ancient times the ash has been revered as a sacred tree, since it cured diseases and could be used for divination and charms. The wood from the ash is also used for the coven stang, or staff, and represents the Horned God. Dressed with garlands and with crossed arrows, the stang is used as an altar; a pitchfork is often used as a substitute.

The leaves can be gathered in early summer and dried for use as a laxative especially in a case where griping pains must be avoided. They have been used to ease colic and pass kidney stones, as well as treating gout, rheumatism, jaundice and relieve flatulence. To be rid of warts, simply prick each one with a new silver pin, then stick the pins into the bark of a living ash tree as you recite: 'Ashen tree, ashen tree, Pray buy these warts off me.'

Ash leaves can be used in any rites of magical regeneration. For 'negative' magic they can be used to remove personal attractiveness of a victim and deny them the support and well wishing of even their closest friends and family. In extreme cases, a blend of incense from ash leaves can be used to break any loving links, partnerships and friendships. A brew of ash keys can also help to unlock the door between the worlds before any shamanic journeying. They can also be used in rituals to gain wealth and prosperity, and if burnt at the Winter Solstice, will ensure a prosperous coming year for the household.

Ash wood is particularly useful in protective rites and can be used in incense or carried in charm bags. Ash wood can be cut at any time appropriate for magical working (waxing moon for growth; waning moon for diminishing) but there are times when the wood is especially potent — at Midsummer, or when the sun or moon is in the sign of Taurus. Ash twigs or wands are also believed to give the bearer protection from snakes.

## A Witch's Talisman

*'If your lover has forsaken you, and you want to bring him (or her) back to you, take a live pigeon, pluck out its heart, and stick pins therein. Put the heart under your pillow, and your lover will return to you.'* The feathers from the pigeon and the pheasant can be used for making amulets and talismans using less drastic measures. If we don't like the idea of shooting our own dinner, discarded feathers from both birds are easily acquired from woods and hedgerows where the birds roost and preen. Blue pigeon feathers are especially useful in love charms since the dove is sacred to Venus. Combined with the gold plumage of the pheasant, this talisman can be used as a charm that requires binding together male/female, lunar/solar energies.

Chapter Four

# March — Awakening Moon

March is the time for the Awakening Moon when spring sunshine and plants are beginning to appear — represented by the Alder, the tree sacred to Eostre and Bran, the old British raven-god. An early name was *Lide*, derived from the Old English *Hlyda*, which refers to the loudness of the wind during March. The word survived in a country proverb that recommended the eating of 'leeks in Lide and ramsins (wild garlic) in May'. The Norsemen regarded the month as 'the lengthening month that wakes the alder and blooms the whin (gorse)', calling it *Lenct* — meaning Spring. It was a period of enforced fasting when winter stores were running low and as such was incorporated into the church calendar and renamed Lent. The Anglo-Saxons referred to it as *Lenetmonath* or Length-Month as the days were beginning to grow longer. In the 14th century misericord calendar, it was shown as the time for sowing. The Spring Equinox falls on or around 21st.

'The day dawned with a blue sky flecked with puffs of fracto-cumulus cloud tinged with pink, and a sudden din of birdsong as each species staked out territories. Spring had arrived ...' wrote Michael Allaby in *A Year in the Life of a Field*. Although March is usually regarded as the first month of spring, astronomically it straddles the seasons, with the first 20 days belonging to winter.

March was the first month in the old Roman calendar; even in England, it was regarded as the first month of the year and until the calendar changes in 1752, the legal year was reckoned from the 25th March. Nevertheless, we have now reached the turning point between winter and spring — the Vernal or Spring

Equinox. This is a powerful time of the year and marks the moment when the Sun crosses the celestial equator, moving from south to north. For the next six months, it will stay in the northern hemisphere of the sky before crossing the equator (Autumnal Equinox) and returning to the south. For the traditional witch, this is one of the most uncertain and powerful tides in the natural calendar, and probably the original pagan spring fire-festival.

The Feast of Sheela-na-Gig (acknowledged as a symbol of fertility and of gateways between the worlds), falls on 18th. This is a naked female figure, squatting facing the viewer with legs spread open to reveal its exaggerated genitalia. The majority of these are weird little characters dating from early medieval times, and can be found on buildings of the period right across Europe. The Sheelas appeared to have been absorbed into native Irish belief as powerful female protectors but there is little evidence that they are viewed as images of any indigenous pagan deity. An old superstition claims bad luck can be averted by making obsequies to a Sheela by touching her genitals.

The Romans would also have brought the Feast of Luna (31st), goddess of the Moon with them. She was worshipped every year in a special rite at her temple on the Aventine Hill in Rome but similar rites would have taken place in Britain during the Roman occupation. Depending on the phase of the moon to fall on this day, pay your own homage to the goddess.

The dampness of the English spring doesn't stop the alder, one of our most sacred of trees, from flowering during March and April, in fact, the trees are found growing by the waterside some actually growing *in* the water — bearing both catkins (male) and cones (female). The male catkins are greenish in colour and come before the leaves. The female catkins form in small clusters and resemble very small red-brown cones although the tree does not produce any seeds until it has passed its twentieth year. The wood is soft and light in weight, the living wood being white: once cut, however, it shows red and dries to a pinkish hue resembling blood.

Incense made from alder can be used to celebrate the Feast of Ceadda (2nd March), a Celtic deity associated with sacred springs and wells. The Celts revered springs, brooks and streams, and paid an annual tribute to them, often placing the severed heads of their enemies in the water. The traditional witch can make a pilgrimage to draw water from a sacred well or spring and, if necessary, take the time to clear the watercourse of the debris that has accumulated during the winter. Leave a coin bearing the image of a head in tribute.

In the hedgerows, wild plants begin to unfurl and on the bare, black branches of the blackthorn, sprays of white blossom will soon begin to appear, although their premature blossoming in March may herald another snap of cold weather to come — known a 'blackthorn winter'. The blackthorn is a deciduous shrub, common throughout the British Isles and an important wood in traditional witchcraft (see **October**). It does grow in woodland but because it needs plenty of light, it is unlikely to be found under dense cover, preferring the edges of woods, clearings, verges, grassy tracks, hedgerows, embankments and common land. This is a rigid bush with a tangle of vicious spikes that offers nesting birds a large degree of protection from predators. The bark is usually black — hence its name — and in some years the profusion of white starry blossom completely obscures the stem. The small leaves unfurl in May to complete an almost impenetrable hedge or thicket, especially in cold, exposed, or coastal areas.

The clustered blooms of the wych elm glow crimson in the spring sunlight despite the fact that many of the trees have been ravaged by disease, which causes the branches to come crashing down. The name wych, means springy or 'switchy', and refers to its whip-like qualities that made it a useful replacement for English and Welsh longbows when yew was unavailable.

In March, the silver catkins of the pussy willow (see **April**) can be found among the hedgerows and broad-leaved woodland. The tree has been associated since Tudor times with a cure for rheumatism, a crude herbal cure that involved the use of salicylic acid; this was later refined by Edward Stone in the 18th century, and is used today as the basis of the drug aspirin.

### Tincture of Willow *(Salix alba)*

Use willow bark to reduce high fevers and to relieve the pain of arthritis and headaches. Dosage and preparation Tincture — 1 part herb to 5 parts liquid (25% alcohol). Maximum dosage: 1 teaspoon three times a day for adults.

Tinctures are alcohol-based extracts and are taken in much smaller doses than teas or decoctions. The alcohol can extract a wider range of plant chemicals than water and, stored correctly, will keep for up to three years. Put 1 lb fresh chopped bark into a large jar with liquid (as above). Close the jar tightly and keep in a warm place for two weeks, shaking well once a day. Strain off the liquid through muslin and decant into a dark glass bottle. Label and store in a cool place away from sunlight until ready to use. Often has fewer side effects than aspirin.

Hedgerows are now a tangle of woody stems through which the smaller plants have not yet appeared. Already identifiable are oak, holly, thorn and bramble, as well as gorse, and dense growths of ivy and woodbine. The foxgloves are in leaf but have not yet produced new stems, and look like large primrose plants.

Ground ivy, which is actually a member of the mint family, begins to creep among the tree roots in hedges and waste ground, showing its purple flowers from March to May. Its bitter taste was used to clear ale and give it a strong, bitter flavour, remaining the major flavouring ingredient in brewing until the introduction of the hop in the 16th century. Culpeper wrote of it in his herbal: 'It is good to tun up with new drink, for it will clarify it in a night, that it will be fit to drinke the next morning; if any drinke be thick with removing, it will do the like in a few hours.' Old ale containing ground ivy was recorded by 'ale conners', established by William the Conqueror to assess the quality of brewing. In Georgian England, the plant was believed to be a good treatment for the damaged eyes of fighting cocks, and an old country remedy consisting of ground ivy leaves, honey, sugar and boiling water was claimed to cure coughs and colds.

On the banks of the stream and in the water meadows, marsh marigolds and lady's smock burst into bloom. The flower's name, *smock*, originally had a crude sexual connotation and for this reason it was considered unsuitable for inclusion in the garlands that decorated the churches, so it's highly appropriate for pagan rituals! During the Victorian era, it underwent a conversion and was dedicated to the Virgin Mary in order to rid the plant of its vulgar history. Marsh marigolds, or to give them their more popular name, kingcups have been growing in this country since long before the Ice Age. The leaves can cause painful blistering if they remain in contact with bare skin and the Saxons applied the leaves to carbuncles as a counter-irritant.

*Ladysmocks silver, kingcups gold,*
*These are the meadow's wealth untold.*
*Gleaming in sunlight, a joy to behold...*

The flowers are ideal for use in a 'money' spell as they represent 'gold and silver' and the poem can be adapted to use as a chant while spell-casting.

The native brown hare is sighted more frequently during March, and for the traditional witch the animal doesn't bode ill as it has done for our country neighbours throughout the centuries. The reason for this is because throughout the pre-Roman era it was looked upon as a holy creature, associated with fertility and the returning spring. Divinations were taken from its movements and ordinary men *never* ate its flesh. For the Anglo-Saxons the *hāra* (hare) was revered as the sacred animal of Eostre, the goddess of springtime, and many of the later traditional hare-hunts obviously have their roots in the concept of the animal being a sacred spring beast. By Norman times, however, the hare's speed and dexterity demonstrated during the hunt earned it the dubious honour of being classed as 'one of the four *Beasts of Venery*'. These animals — which also included the hart (deer), the boar and the wolf — were considered by the nobility to be the only creatures worthy of the chase, and honoured accordingly.

The long bat-like ears are part of the hare's early-warning system, picking up the slightest sound. Teamed with a pair of eyes set on the side of its head (they can also look backwards), it means that nothing can take a wily hare by surprise — unless these faculties become impaired by ill health or age. Contrary to popular belief that scenes of the Mad March Hare are mating rituals (a hare may have up to *four* litters a year), many of those boxing hares packing a punch are females! They also have a taste for blackthorn twigs. To watch them, take a good, strong black-thorn stem, or one shot with twigs and stick it firmly in the ground in the open field. The smell of blackthorn will draw the hare to the spot and he will move around nibbling the twigs.

Added to this, all over the world from ancient times, 'the hare is a symbol of enlightenment, not only of the spirit but of the dawn, the dawn of the day and the dawn of the year which we call spring,' wrote George Ewart Evans in *The Leaping Hare*. 'In Europe hares had existed for about a million years before [man], and at least in the legends concerning the moon they appear in the most ancient mythology of all.'

If you want to understand which animals and birds inhabit the fields and hedgerows look at the tracks in the mud; in dry weather look for the footprints where birds and animals go to drink at a puddle, in a tractor rut or stream bank. The inhabitants of the animal world are now busy looking for suitable breeding places and food supplies — the blackbird being among the first to build its nest and by the end of the month, the first clutch of eggs may have hatched.

It is when we watch the lambs in the fields that the more spiritually aware will come to understand that to face every day the brutality of Nature isn't necessarily brutalising, and that the suffering of animals rend the hearts of farmers, too. As Stephen Budiansky observes in *The Covenant of the Wild*, farmers deal with tragedy not by closing their hearts to the suffering within Nature but by opening their minds to the larger truth of Nature. He explains that farmers understand that even in their little tame corner of the natural world, that Nature is a force larger than themselves, with its own rhythms, its own purpose, its own sense of morality that makes a mockery of man's. 'They still cared and struggled to save a dying lamb … and when the time came for it to die, they still packed it off to market …' It is a lesson in how much we have simply forgotten in our civilised lives, where the harsh rules of Nature almost never intrude.

## The Hearth Fire

This is a good old-fashioned recipe to take away the cold and damp, following a long walk in the fields and along the hedgerows; and a typical example of farmhouse kitchen cookery that would have been prepared in many a witch's cauldron down through the ages.

## Pot-Luck

¾ *lb beef or mutton*
2 *teaspoons flour*
*Salt and pepper to taste*
1½ *lb potatoes*
2 *carrots*
2 *pints water*

*3 onions*
*½ dessertspoon beef dripping*

Trim and remove all fat from the meat and cut into small pieces about ½ inch square. Dip in flour seasoned with pepper and salt. Peel and slice the onions. Peel the potatoes and cut into quarters if they are small or into eighths if they are large. When all ingredients are prepared, grease a casserole. Put a layer of sliced onion in the bottom and cover with a layer of meat, then a layer of potato. Repeat these layers, taking care that the top layer is potato. If liked, each layer of potatoes can be seasoned to taste with pepper and salt. Add water and dab the potatoes with beef dripping. Cover the casserole and cook in a moderate oven till boiling. Reduce the heat and simmer for 2 hours. About 20 minutes before serving remove the lid so that the potatoes can brown. Serve from the dish.

Wild foods are still in short supply but the coltsfoot and lesser celandine can be used to prepare salves and ointments. The lesser celandine or pilewort has been used for centuries to cure haemorrhoids; coltsfoot leaves can be eaten raw in salads, added to soups and cooked as a vegetable, as well as having numerous medicinal uses.

**Weatherwise**
In March, the countryside begins its transition from brown to green, with windy and dry weather generally considered to be a good thing:

- *March winds and April showers bring forth May flowers*
- *A bushel of March dust is worth a king's ransom*
- *A dry and cold March never begs for bread*

There is some contradiction in the weather lore. The saying that

March comes in like a lion and goes out like a lamb, gives the lie to a popular rhyme about the borrowing days (either the last three days of March or the first three days of April):

*March borrowed from April*
*Three days and they were ill*
*The first was snow and sleet*
*The next was cold and wet*
*The third was a freeze*
*The bird's nests stuck to trees*

March is often not a pleasant month and has been described as the month God designed to show those who don't drink what a hangover is like! For the traditional witch, however, the power of the March winds is an added impetus for magical working.

**The Turning of the Year**
This is a month of amazing contrasts, with weather ranging from brilliant sunny days to deep snow, gale-force winds or warm breezes, gentle showers or icy rain. Because of the uncertain weather conditions, young leaves and flowers that have unfurled in the sunshine can be blighted by severe frost a day later.

**Then:** Sowing.
**Now:** Snow covers the tender young crops.

**The Circle rite for the month should ask a blessing on the house for the coming year.** At the Spring Equinox repeat the burning of the traditional nine sacred woods in a bundle (ash, birch, yew, hazel, rowan, willow, pine, hawthorn and blackthorn) and sprinkle the ash from the fire around the main entrance to the house.

## Alder Magic

With the alder's natural habitat being streams and riverbanks it is not surprising that it can be viewed as being sacred to Elemental Water, although with its various associations, it seems to embrace all four elements. Pipes and whistles were made from alder, making it sacred to Pan and Elemental Air; whistles can be used magically to conjure up destructive winds — especially from the North (Elemental Earth). Associated with the Elemental Fires of the smith-gods (because although it burns poorly, it makes one of the best charcoals) it has the powers of both dissolution and regeneration. Primarily, the alder is the tree of fire, using the power of fire to free the earth from water and a symbol of resurrection, as its blooms heralds the drying up of the winter floods by the Spring Sun. Use alder as part of your magical workings at Spring Equinox

The indigenous British thought that the tree possessed 'human' qualities when they first witnessed the white timber turning a vivid reddish-orange — the colour of blood — which caused it to be revered as a sentinel, guarding the realms of Otherworld. Originally, it was one of the sacred British trees but was displaced by the ash following the 'Battle of the Trees', which means that it was sacred long before the Celts came to these islands. It is described as 'the very battle-witch of all woods, tree that is hottest in the fight'.

Used as incense, alder is used to disperse other powers and to dissolve malevolent forces. When burnt, it can also cause dissention between even the closest of relationships and the felling of a sacred alder will be revenged by fire in the home. The alder also was used for its fine dyes: red from its bark, green from its flowers, brown from its twigs, with the green dye has long been associated in British folklore with the green clothes of the Faere Folk. Hang a sprig in your home and alder brings you and yours under the protection of powerful forces, which will both attract good fortune and banish negative powers.

Chapter Five

# The Witch's Field

In 1976, Britain experienced the hottest, driest summer for a hundred years. The grass scorched, crops failed, and even trees began to suffer as the water level fell away. So extreme was the drought that for the first time archaeological features deep in the subsoil beneath lowland arable fields became visible from the air as cropmarks. Deep-rooted plants, finding water in long-buried ditches and pits, remained green while their neighbours were burned brown, and the outlines of whole field systems and settlements reappeared, briefly mapped out in green on the parched landscape. The pattern revealed was of prehistoric lowland agriculture on a vast scale.

And if the woods are the traditional witch's temple, then the man-made enclosures of neatly patterned fields, are the traditional witch's tool-shed. These first changes took place about 4500 years ago, when early man began to clear the forest that covered most of the country, and created small, rectangular fields bounded by earth banks in which grew wheat and barley. Traces of New Stone Age fields can still be seen around Dartmoor, on White Ridge and Standon Down. Here the fields are small, circular clearances about an acre in size, which were cleared of stones and scrub, then hoed with sticks to plant corn.

By the time of the Roman invasion, farming had become established, with as many as four million acres under cultivation. In the 1st century BC, British agriculture was generating a grain surplus that was traded on the European market — the culmination of centuries of large-scale clearance and cultivation, which had began in the late Stone Age. When the Romans left, the land reverted to wilderness, and when the Anglo-Saxons arrived, they had to clear heavily forested river valleys.

The fields in which a witch walks today, however, are enclosures made largely in the 100 years between 1750 and 1850 to exploit new methods of farming, although traces of the old 'open' system can still be seen in fields where the surface appears to be folded in gigantic corrugations. The small fields in the southwest, especially Cornwall, owe their odd shapes to the ground configuration, and probably the efforts of the Celtic farmers. Of particular interest to the witch are the boulders, trees and streams that have all served to denote the limits of land ownership, and from early times these *natural features* were supplemented by man-made markers, including banks, ditches, walls, hedges and tracks. These boundaries mark the magical division between time and place — **the place of time between times.**

Stand at a field gate at any time of the year and chart the progress of the seasons as the stark, bare twigs of winter gradually develop the soft bloom of green in spring.

Early summer offers a profusion of creamy blossoms covering lush greenery that will slowly ripen into splashes of purple and scarlet berries. With the coming of autumn, the leaves of the field maple will glisten golden in the sunlight, followed by a dazzling palette of reds, and bronzes and yellows ... to be replaced by branches glistening white with hoare-frost or snow at Midwinter.

The field gate also offers a vantage point from which to observe the changing patterns in the weather. Clouds, for example, have been described as 'Nature's poetry for dreamers' and that contemplating them benefits the soul. Gavin Pretor-Pinney, author of *The Cloudspotter's Guide* maintains that cloud watching is more about a person's philosophical disposition than any geographical location. 'Because of the stately pace in which clouds move and the gradual rate at which they develop, contemplating them is akin to meditation,"' he says. 'The mere act of sitting, watching and observing slows you down to their pace.'

On a magical level, we can use the ancient Greek method of divination (nephelomancy — from the Greek *nephele*) from the patterns seen in cloud formations. This means the witch intuitively interpreting cloud configurations to answer questions or predict a future outcome. As with other methods that use patterns and requiring translation by psychic means, the symbols in the sky can be interpreted in many ways with certain images being highly significant to different individuals. And a solitary witch leaning on a farm gate, seemingly staring across a meadow, will not draw attention, despite the fact that there are magical doings afoot!

A true meadow is a field in which the grasses and other plants are allowed to grow up in the summer and then cut for hay — the traditional way of obtaining winter feed for livestock, and again, this process has been carried out for centuries. Today, although there are few ancient meadows that have never been ploughed, drained or fertilized, many have always been used as hayfields and have a profusion of wild flowers and grasses associated with traditional meadowland. These are the signs the witch needs to be able to recognise — the types of grass found in old meadows including sweet vernal grass. This is an early flowerer and its foliage is strongly scented with a substance called *coumarin*, which is what gives new-mown hay its sweet smell. To know that the beautiful buttercup meadow is poisonous to cattle ... but once the hay is cut and dried the buttercups lose their poison and can be eaten with the grasses.

A modern witch should never expect a field that is part of a working farm to support so rich a flora and fauna as one that is not, but according to Michael Allaby's observations in his *A Year In The Life Of A Field*, there is a large population of species that shares a field with the grass, clover and livestock, 'and even the most apparently insignificant of creatures is adapted to the circumstances in which it lives'. The witch knows that human affairs still count for little here, and 'our arbitrary marking of the passage of time means nothing where the cycle of life is endlessly repeated'.

Our chosen field and hedgerow focuses our attention on a small piece of the landscape — it may be a familiar field walk, or a long track that meanders between high banks and tangled hedgerows. It may even be a local park or playing field. Or, if we have no access to the great tangle of the wild hedgerow, it can be recreated on the astral where we can visit whenever we choose.

NB: Fields in Britain are measured in acres (4840 square yards) and hectares (approx 120 square yards). The acre was a measure of a long strip of land fixed by Edward I in 1305, and based on the amount of land a man could plough with two oxen in a day. For ease of reckoning, a football pitch is about 1¾ acres. The hectare is a metric unit of square measure, equal to about 2½ acres now adopted by land agents.

## Pathworking Exercise

Within traditional witchcraft one of the most potent times for magical or meditational working is at dawn and dusk. As we have seen, of particular interest to the witch are the boulders, trees and streams that serve to denote the limits of land ownership, and often supplemented by man-made markers, including banks, ditches, walls, double-hedges and tracks. These boundaries mark the magical division between time and place — **the place of time between times**, and it is here we will attempt our next exercise. Gone are the days when we could roam the countryside at any time of the day, or we may not have physical access, so we can perform this psychic exercise in the safety of the home.

Firstly, we need to visualise a 'field margin' that we can recreate on the astral at any time. It may be a favourite spot a where the field is flanked by a stream; a large boulder in the over-grown margin, moved to its present location by glaciers in the last Ice Age; or the green cave of a double hedge. Our picture book will provide us with images that can focus the mind's eye like a camera lens as we stand at the edge of a wood, looking out to where mist still lingers over the stubble field; an avenue of beech trees; or a winding cart track between tall banks of wild flowers. This is our 'jumping off' point where we can visualise ourselves before embarking on a pathworking.

Pathworking is an astral journey for the **purpose of magical/mystical instruction** whereby the witch has no control over the outcome or sequence of events. This state is usually reached via visualisation where the witch sets the scene on a *conscious* level and then allows herself to be drawn into an involuntary journey of discovery and/or revelation. So ... at dusk or dawn, make yourself comfortable and set up your Circle according to your own working method, and begin by visualising your chosen 'field margin'. Concentrate on the images before you and allow yourself to be drawn into the scene ...

No one can predict the results of a pathworking, or where the journey will lead, since each individual's results will be different. Much depends, however, on what we have in our mind *prior* to the pathworking, and this will influence the direction or outcome.

Since we are using the technique in search of magical or mystical instruction, it should not be used for a personal gratification or mere thrill seeking. Remember to ensure you are properly 'earthed' when returning from any pathworking by consuming sweet biscuits and a warm drink, since nothing dispels psychic energy like food!

## A Witch's Easter Rite

*To this pool the people would come on Easter morning to see the sun dance and play in the water ... others would put out buckets of water, or gather by large bodies of water to see the sun dance's reflection ....* To witness the phenomena was believed to grant the viewer health and happiness for the coming year, and the witch should take herself off to a sacred pool, spring or lake on the first Sunday following the full moon after the Spring Equinox. It is said that those who cannot see the performance are lacking in faith in the Old Ones.

Chapter Six

# April — Grass Moon

April is referred to as the Grass Moon when pasture lands are glowing green with fresh grazing — represented by the Willow. This was a tree of mourning in the old days and is often referred to as such in traditional folksongs and ballads, although catkins gathered on May Day bring good luck. The Anglo-Saxon called this time *Eosturmonath* or 'Goddess-month' while the Irish-Gaelic and Scottish-Gaelic for May Eve is *Beltaine*. April is also a Roman word from the Latin *aperire*, a word describing the opening of a leaf. In the 14th century misericord calendar, it was shown as the time for scaring birds from the fields.

April is the month when spring really begins to make its presence felt. Deciduous trees produce new leaves and blossom; wild flowers appear in the woods and hedgerows. Birds build their nests and fill the air with song — in pagan times, the rebirth of nature was celebrated by honouring the pagan goddess, Eostre, whose voice could be heard once again in the 'continual stir of bees, and in the call of the cuckoo'.

Even town-based witches will be able to recognise the unmistakeable sound of the cuckoo. Cuckoos are found almost everywhere, but tend to avoid built-up areas. They are most common on mixed farmland and around water, particularly in the South and Midlands. The male's distinctive call (a female cuckoo has a 'bubbling cry') carries long distances, usually starting around Easter and continuing well into July. As with most birds, they are usually noisiest earlier in the day, particularly between dawn and mid-morning.

There are numerous superstitions relating to the bird — girls may ask it when they will marry, or old men when they will die, and the calls that follow indicate the number of years each must wait. When you first hear the call of the cuckoo, turn over the money in your pocket to ensure riches to come in the next twelve-month, or make a wish. If the call comes from your right, you will have good luck, but if it comes from the left the results will be negative.

In Wales, it is considered unlucky to hear the bird's call before the 6th April; very lucky to hear it first on 28th April, and unlucky to hear it after old Midsummer Day. To hear the cuckoo after August is an extremely bad omen hence:

*In April, come he will,*
*In May, he sings all day,*
*In June, he changes his tune,*
*In July, he prepares to fly,*
*In August, go he must.*

In many parts of the country the bird's first appearance and departure regulated the dates of local fairs, such as Heathfield Fair (Sussex); Sawbridgeworth Spring Fair, Orleton and Brampton Bryan Fairs (Hertfordshire); Tenbury and Pershore Fairs (Worcestershire).

The date for Easter is still fixed by the lunar calendar, with Easter Sunday falling on the first Sunday after the full moon, following the Spring Equinox. The giving and receiving of eggs is nowadays associated with the Christian festival of that name — although *both* elements are pagan in origin. The hare, also associated with Eostre was considered unlucky and identified as a witches' familiar, and as a result became the 'Easter Bunny'!

A great deal of country-lore revolves around the affects the moon has on sowing and harvesting. Good Friday was traditionally the time for planting potatoes although many countrymen would say this should be done at the waxing or full moon. *A Dictionary of Superstitions* cites recorded instances from 77AD to the present day that confirm that all vegetables should be cut, gathered and stored while the moon is on the wane. Many farmers and rural gardeners still only plant corn and seeds during the waxing or full moon, since it is believed that nothing will thrive if you plant when the moon is on the wane.

By now, the hedgerows will be bursting into leaf to provide cover for a wide variety of birds, animals and insects. During April, the five-petalled flowers of the blackthorn break into a cloud of white, covering the shrub's bare branches in the hedgerow. This is the easy method of telling the difference between the black and whitethorn: blackthorn flowers first on bare branches, while white or hawthorn flowers after the leaves have broken. The cold spring weather stops the leaves of the blackthorn from unfurling thereby creating the wonderful contrast of creamy-white blossom, with its own delicate perfume, against the ebony wood. In the autumn, the leaves will turn from crimson, to purple to gold.

### The Unpopular Poplar

The poplar is another native tree that doesn't appear in the Tree Alphabet, though the related aspen does. This is surprising because the red catkins would have drawn attention to the leafless tree in the spring. Many rural superstitions associate the poplar with the same Christian mythic over-lay as the aspen and in some places it shares the same name as 'shivver-tree' because of its trembling leaves. It also shares the aspen's ability to cure agues and fever. A Lincolnshire remedy states that a sufferer should cut off a lock of hair and wrap it around a branch of a poplar tree saying:

*My aches and pains thou now must take,*
*Instead of me I bid thee shake.*

He or she should then go straight home, speaking to no one on the way, after that they will be free from ague forever. Some sources state that it is necessary to fast for twelve hours before attempting this charm.

The black poplar is a fine, tall tree and, like the alder, is another lover of moisture. It may be found growing in damp meadows, keeping, if it can, close to a ditch or stream, where its long roots can stretch out to their full extent, water-seeking as they go. The sticky, sharp-pointed yellowish buds of the red male catkins appear in winter, developing into long hanging catkins. The flowers add a touch of colour to the bare countryside for just a couple of days in early April, before the leaves begin to break. These fall to the ground before the shooting of the glossy, heart-shaped leaves and are known in some areas as the Devil's Fingers, where it is believed to be unlucky to pick them up. The fluffy catkins on the female tree produce a white down that drifts away like fragments of cotton wool; the tree retains its flowers as these form the fruit that ripens in May.

Poplars are closely related to willows and the bark also contains salicin, which reduces inflammation and relieves pain. Medicinally it is used internally for rheumatoid arthritis, gout, fevers, lower back pain, urinary complaints, digestive and liver disorders, debility and anorexia. Externally it can be used to treat chilblains, haemorrhoids, infected wounds and sprains. Older cures include using the juice to ease earache, while the crushed buds, mixed with honey were given as treatment for sore eyes. An ointment dating back to medieval times, which included poplar buds as the main ingredient was used for reducing inflammation and bruising.

## Witches' Flying Ointment

It is known how some of these flying ointments were made because a number of English and Continental writers in the 16th and 17th centuries described the methods. All the recipes contained extracts from strongly poisonous plant such as aconite, deadly nightshade and hemlock, together with cinquefoil, sweet flag, poplar leaves and parsley, mixed with soot and some sort of oil as a fixing agent.

Apple blossom in the hedgerows is always a welcome sign of spring. The crab apple blooms in late April and must surely be the real 'goddess' tree of the British Isles (see **September**). It usually occurs singly, scattered throughout almost all types of woodland and hedgerow and, according to Oliver Rackham in *Trees and Woodland in the British Landscape*, there were roughly one tree for every ten acres in the 1970s. Crab apple blossom is pinkish-white with an exquisite and delicate perfume; the fruit is small, ranging in colour from yellow to red, with a very sharp taste.

The saying 'an apple a day keeps the doctor away' lays claim to the fruit's health-giving qualities that science now recognises as having more than a grain of truth. In medieval times, the fruit was a cure-all; the bark was also used medicinally. The fruit was mainly used to relieve constipation, reduce acidity of the stomach and assist the digestion. Rotten apples were used as a relief for sore eyes. Prehistoric man is known to have eaten wild apples and to have used them to make a primitive form of cider, although our native wild apple (*malus pumila*), is a small, hard, sour fruit. The cultivated variety of apple, however, was probably introduced into Britain by the Romans and it is believed that the indigenous crab apple blossom was white — the pinkish hue being a corruption of the cultivated variety of apple. During medieval times, the monks increased the number of varieties of 'eating' apple, which became a favourite fruit eaten cooked or raw. Wild apples were also used for making cider, chutneys, sauces, jams and jellies.

From May to September the hedges will also be a mass of the pink and white flowers of the bramble ... the leaves were once placed on inflammations to reduce swelling and an orange dye made from the roots. There are, in fact, several hundred species of blackberry found in the British Isles, each with its own characteristic pattern of thorn, leaf shape, flower colour, fruit shape and taste. And although hedges, wasteland and heaths abound with blackberries in the autumn, some are not as good to eat as others.

From May to September, the stream that runs along the side of the meadow is fringed with water forget-me-nots in wet shady places. These tiny blue flowers were worn as symbols of love by young people in the Middle Ages, and can still be used in spells or charms for romance. A fast-running stream is also useful for a witch in disposing of spells and charms that are past their 'sell-by date'. It has long been believed that 'magic' cannot cross a stream or river, and any old charms that need disposing of should be broken up and the individual ingredients cast into the fast running water to disperse any residue of magical energy.

Similarly, water from a dew pond can also be incorporated into magical workings.

This is a natural, or sometimes man-made hollow, supplied with water by mist. Traditional witches consider them to be places of natural energy and the water can be used in magical workings that require an Otherworld element.

In some sheltered spots, cowslips will begin to show through in meadows, pastures and banks. The flower's Old English name of *cuslippe* meaning cowpat, reflects the Saxon belief that it grew from cow dung. These pretty little key-shaped yellow flowers once grew in profusion in meadowland across England and Wales but its numbers have been reduced drastically in the past fifty years. This used to be a favourite flower among country folk and is a member of the primrose family — sometimes called the 'paigle'. The flowers are deep yellow with orange spots, flowering in early summer with a head of drooping flowers. The cowslip should not be mistaken for the oxlip that flowers in early spring, and which is mainly found in southeastern England.

Flowers collected from 'cowslip meadows' in May or June make a delicate wine, once recommended as a cure for insomnia; while ointment made from cowslips was claimed to remove spots and wrinkles. Cowslip wine was popular in most rural pantries but it is now illegal to pick the flowers, and so the following has been included merely for interest sake:

## Cow Slip Wine
*4 quarts of cowslip flowers*
*4 quarts of water*
*3 lb loaf sugar*
*finely grated rind and juice*
*of one orange and one lemon.*
*2 tablespoonfuls of brewers' yeast*
*or ¼ of an oz of compressed yeast moistened with water,*
*¼ pint brandy if liked*

Boil the sugar and water together for about half an hour, skimming when necessary. Pour, still boiling, over the rinds and strained juice of the orange and lemon. Let it cool, then stir in the yeast and cowslip flowers, cover with a cloth, and allow to remain undisturbed for 48 hours. Turn the whole into a clean, dry cask, add the brandy, bung tightly and let it remain thus for 8 weeks. Draw off into clean, dry bottles. Cork securely and store in a cool, dry place for about 3-4 weeks, then the wine will be ready for use.

This month the hedgehog emerges from its watertight nest of grass and moss. Once its hunger is satisfied, it will only emerge at twilight to locate food; at dawn it rolls into a tight ball protected by its spines. Hedgehogs go into such a deep sleep that the animal's loud snoring and snuffling can be heard quite clearly. They also make a low whistling sound when they first come out at night and two hedgehogs fighting in the undergrowth can sound like a small child moaning. This small animal is deceptively agile being capable of climbing trees to take fledglings and eggs and is a good swimmer. An Anglo-Roman proverb commenting on the hedgehog's armour says: 'The fox has many tricks, the hedgehog only one; and that is greater than them all.' Foxes have been known, however, to roll the hedgehog into water so that it has to uncurl to swim and so becomes defenceless. Nevertheless, this is another animal with which the traditional witch might identify.

Grass snakes also emerge from hibernation during late March and early April. In Celtic times, the *snaca* was regarded as a holy creature and revered as the serpent of the water spirits, acting as a protector of sacred wells and guardian of holy springs. It is Britain's largest snake and females can reach up to nearly six foot, although the more normal length is three to four feet. It was the grass snake that provided the skin for the traditional witch's garter.

## The Hearth Fire

Easter Lamb is a traditional dish all over Europe and this one is a Welsh recipe because good Welsh lamb is the finest meat available for spring roasting.

### Honeyed Welsh Lamb (Oen Cymreig Melog)

*3-4 lb joint or shoulder of spring lamb*
*1 cup of thick honey*
*½ pint cider*
*Salt and pepper*
*1 teaspoon ginger*
*2 sprigs of fresh rosemary*

Use a roasting dish lined with baking foil in which the joint will fit snugly. Rub salt, pepper and ginger all over the joint and insert the fresh rosemary into deep cuts in the meat. Coat the skin with honey and pour cider around the joint. Allowing 30 minutes to the lb, roast near the top of a moderate oven Gas 6 (400F/200C) for half an hour. Baste the meat and reduce heat to Gas 4 (350F/180C) for the remainder of the cooking time. Baste every 20 minutes and add extra cider if necessary. Serve the sauce separately in a warmed gravy boat.

The fields and woods are now full of surprisingly tasty 'wild' salad vegetables. Try wild garlic leaves, chickweed, clover, sorrel, sow thistle, lamb's lettuce or burnet. And as a different slant on traditional mint sauce, chop the leaves of jack-by-the-hedge with hawthorn buds and a little mint, mix well with vinegar and sugar.

In April, the nutty-tasting young leaves of the hawthorn are delicious in salads; and can also be added to cheese on toast, or used with bacon to make a savoury roll.

Roll out some suet pastry, cover with young hawthorn leaves and strips of bacon, season and roll up. Steam in a cloth for at least an hour and serve sliced with gravy.

Or make hawthorn flower liqueur by filling a wide-necked bottle with the flowers (with the stalks removed), sprinkle with two-tablespoons of sugar, and cover with brandy. Keep for at least three months, shaking occasionally. Strain and seal before drinking.

The common stinging nettle is the second most common wild plant in Britain and taking over more and more of the countryside. Although they are looked upon as a troublesome weed, they are an infallible sign of rich, fertile soil and thrive around rabbit warrens and badger sets. To grow well nettles need a good 'dollop' of animal phosphate from bones or dung, or river silt. Pick the young tips to make a fresh, tangy soup, using potato and onion as a base. Or brew up with water, sugar and yeast to make nettle beer, perfect for the summer months. Don't use the leaves after July, however, or you will be spending a lot of unnecessary time in the lavatory! And where there are nettles, there will be dock leaves to sooth the sting. These are over four inches wide with blunt tips and were used to wrap butter to keep it fresh.

## And for health

*A purging ale, to be taken in April. Take the strongest ale you can get, and leave it in a bag with crushed senna, polpody of the oak, bay-berries, ash-keys, aniseeds and fennel seeds: drink thereof about a pint morning and evening, it purgeth the body mightily.*

Mrs Harrington's Book, 18th century

## Weatherwise

April is known for the unpredictability and changeability of its weather: *April weather, rain and sunshine both together.* The proverbial 'April showers' are welcomed by farmer and gardeners alike, but the month is also notorious for sharp frosts that will nip young plants in the bud. The blossoming of the blackthorn towards the end of the month is often accompanied by a period of unseasonably cold weather — hence a blackthorn winter. Thunder in April is generally regarded as a favourable omen: *When April blows his horn, it's good for hay and corn.*

Daisies flower nearly all the year round and can be found in short grassland everywhere but at night or in very dark weather, the flower head remains completely closed. The flower acts as a light-metre: in full sunshine, the flower heads are fully open. In hazy light, the petals begin to close and in cloudy weather the petals fold to show their external pink tingeing. A witch could impress her neighbours with this casual observation.

## The Turning of the Year

Dawn chorus: the first to break into song in spring and summer is the lark, singing as it soars in the sky. It is soon joined by the blackbird, song thrush, robin, wood pigeon, turtle dove, mistle thrush, willow warbler, wren, chiff-chaff and other birds — roughly in that order. In midsummer this dawn chorus starts before 4am, and is best heard at about 5am when most birds have joined in, with most birds singing from the same perch every morning. Birds sing less in the cold, dark months of the year, so when there is a heavy, overcast sky at daybreak the dawn chorus starts later.

**Then:** Bird scaring from the crops.
**Now:** Growth gets well under way.

**The Circle ritual for April is a very good time to work positively for growth and future plans; for a new life and fresh beginnings.** A Beltaine celebration, like all pagan spring festivals, should always contain an element of flirtation and fun. It is a good time for prophetic dreams and divination — using what you have had in the past in order to maximise the future.

### Willow Magic

There are several different species of willow but they all have similar medicinal properties and can be used interchangeably in magic. Willows are one of the earliest colonisers of these Islands and it should come as no surprise that it can be found in the Celtic tree alphabet; it is classed as one of the Peasant Trees and bears the name *saill*.

In Celtic times, those wishing to learn eloquence, to be granted visions, prophetic dreams or inspiration, frequented groves of willow. Artists and artisans who learned their craft in willow groves were reputed to be especially skilled.

If you are unable to visit a willow grove, collect some of the leaves and bark to make into incense. Use when meditating or pathworking if you are looking for inspiration.

Willow can also be used in love spells and for friendship. Collect the grey 'pussy willow' flowers and place in a charm bag or give a friend a bunch of pussy willow for luck.

For medicinal use, the dried bark of the willow is collected from young branches during the growth period for extracting the aspirin-like substances to help combat high fever and to relieve the pain of arthritis and headaches. Although these claims have not been clinically proven, there is strong evidence that willow bark was used in a similar way to aspirin long before the invention of the drug.

## Decoction
Decoctions are water-based and used for the tough part of herbs, such as seeds, barks and roots, that release their active constituents only when cut or broken into small pieces and simmered. Use 3-5 gm of willow bark per cup of water. Put the herb and water into an enamel pan and bring to the boil slowly and simmer for 15 minutes. Strain and add water to make up a full cup if necessary. Sip slowly while hot and sweeten with honey if required.

Because willow also has 'Otherworld' associations, it is inadvisable to use a willow staff to drive animals since it was believed that these would soon be taken from you and pass down into the underworld, i.e. the herd or flock would die. In folklore, the willow was associated with sorrow and lost love. Sprigs were sometimes worn as a sign of mourning; or by those who had been forsaken in love, hence the words of the old folksong: 'All around my hat I will wear the green willow'.

Because of the willow's association with rivers, it is representative of Elemental Water. It is usually the bark of the tree that is used magically in incense but a bundle of twigs can also be used to concentrate Elemental Fire. The twigs should be lit from a special fire or consecrated candle and then plunged into consecrated water. This is known as a 'fire potion' and can be used for magical cleansing. To increase the potency, add an infusion of the appropriate herb. The potion may be drunk or applied as a compress of cotton wool to increase psychic powers. This is the witch's answer to the blacksmith's 'thunder water'.

### A Witch's Dandelion Recipe

*For liver complaints we dug up dandelion roots with a one-tined fork specially made by the blacksmith for the purpose, washed, dried, and roasted them in the oven, then crushed them to a powder with a bottle, and after pouring boiling water over them, half a teaspoon to large cup, we added milk and sugar, when we had it, and drank the beverage for breakfast as coffee ... We also ate the young dandelion leaves in early spring when there was no other green salad about, sometimes bleaching them, by covering them with an old sack. This was supposed to be a blood-cleanser.* Dandelions can be used today with the young leaves at their best in early summer. Serve as a salad with a dressing of olive oil and lemon juice, or with chopped bacon sautéed in oil with chopped chives and lemon juice, or croutons and a soft-boiled egg.

Chapter Seven

# May — Planting Moon

May is the time of the Planting Moon when seeds were scattered on the earth for harvesting in the autumn — represented by the White-thorn or Hawthorn; also know as the May Tree because of its associations with May Day. Since this is a sacred tree, it was considered unlucky to take branches of flowers of hawthorn into the house; if used as decorations outside it was considered a symbol of good luck. The Irish-Gaelic name for the time is *Beltaine,* which also denotes the festival that takes place on May Eve. In Scottish-Gaelic it is *Cèitean,* which means beginning; this was the first month of summer in the Celtic calendar. The Anglo-Saxon name for the month was *Trimilki,* meaning 'three-milk' because in that month they began to milk their kine three times a day and signifying a time of plenty. In the 14th century misericord calendar, it was shown as the time for blessing the crops.

The saying goes that *'one swallow doesn't a summer make'* but the first sighting of a swallow returning from its South African wintering grounds has a feel of good luck about it. Parents and offspring will return year after year to the same building and, if prevented from entering, will spend hours searching for a way in. Swallows are primarily farmland birds that breed inside buildings, and are probably most common in dairy regions where they are attracted to the insects living around cowpats and cattle barns. From now on, the warm summer evenings will echo to the cries of these agile birds as they skim through the air, catching insects in wide, gaping mouths.

From Anglo-Saxon times it has been considered bad luck to

kill a *swallewe* and it was believed that if a farmer were responsible for the death of one of these birds, or the destruction of its nest, his cows' milk would turn to blood. This has proved *not* to be one of those country-myths, as swallows feed on the insects that cause mastitis in cows: and a symptom of the infection is blood in the milk. Swallows spend much of their time in flight and seldom touch the ground, except for collecting mud to be used for nest building. Each bird returns to the same nesting site every year despite the fact that they are estimated to fly 1.25 million miles during a lifetime.

Although this is traditionally a time for merrymaking, there are some rather gloomy superstitions attached to the month. It is a bad time to marry (*Marry in May, rue for aye*), or to give birth (*May chickens come cheeping*), and May kittens were always believed to be bad mousers. In some parts of the country, it was considered unwise to buy a broom in May, as the purchaser would be suspected of being a witch!

Nevertheless, one of our oldest traditions is dancing around the Maypole to mark the start of summer. The original maypole was a stripped tree erected on the village green as the focal point of May Day celebrations and dancing. This rather risqué poem, *The Maypole*, dating from the 17th century and written by Robert Herrick is an ideal chant for a Beltaine ritual:

## The Maypole

*The maypole is up,*
*Now give me the cup,*
*I'll drink to the garlands around it;*
*But first unto those*
*Whose hands did compose*
*The glory of flowers that crowned it.*

*A health to my girls*
*Whose husbands may earls*

*Or lords be, granting my wishes;*
*And when that ye wed*
*To the bridal bed,*
*Then multiply all, like to fishes.*

According to folklore, this is the month of flowers when the hedgerows resemble gigantic bouquets of creamy blossom of the May trees (or hawthorn) with their exquisite perfume. Hawthorn can be grown from a fruit very easily and planted within the boundary hedge where it can create an impenetrable barrier, or allowed to mature into an impressive tree that produces masses of white flowers. The old techniques of 'hedge laying' which involves almost cutting through the stem of a young hawthorn and weaving into others along the row, is one of the old country crafts vanishing from farm management skills. This is a shame because a hawthorn hedge is a wonderful place for wildlife.

It's debatable whether the old saying: *Cast ne'er a clout/Till May be out* refers to the end of the month itself, or flowering of the May tree, because if the flowering season is late due to bad weather, the hawthorn sometimes fails to appear until almost June. The distinctive 'female' perfume of the may blossom resembles the natural smell of a woman, making the tree her very own as a symbol of a goddess-tree. And in return …

*The fair maid who, the first of May*
*Goes to the fields at break of day*
*And washes in dew from the hawthorne tree,*
*Will ever after handsome be.*

So … the real sign that spring is merging into summer is when this frothy white blossom appears and the hedgerows are scented with its delicate perfume. Although traditionally the flower of Beltaine, with the current climatic changes the tree is more likely to flower in early April, but it is still associated with the sensuality of the May Day celebrations. 'I have heard it credibly reported,' wrote one observer in 1583, 'that of 40 or 100 maids going into the wood ... there have scarcely the third part of them returned home undefiled ...'

Common hawthorn (as opposed to woodland hawthorn) is the variety that prefers open country and in a survey of 658 Anglo-Saxon charters and boundary descriptions, it cropped up far more often than any other tree, including oak. The average lifespan of common hawthorn is between 100 and 200 years, but some historic boundary markers are much older — like the Hethel Old Thorn (or Witch of Hethel) mentioned in a 13th century charter. The most famous, of course, is the Glastonbury Thorn that flowers at Midwinter, as well as blossoming at the normal time of the year.

Medicinally, the hawthorn can rival the elder. Culpeper recommends pounded or bruised and boiled seeds as cures for various internal pains, probably because they and the dried flowers can reduce blood pressure and circulatory problems. A compote of fresh fruits was given as a cure for diarrhoea. 'The seeds in the berries beaten to powder being drunk in wine, are good against the stone and dropsy. The distilled water of the flowers stays the lax. The seeds cleared of the down and bruised, being boiled in wine, are good for inward pains.'

In modern herbalism the properties of some of the hawthorn's active constituents are now better understood and present a remarkable picture of what is known as synergy — meaning 'working together'. Some constituents strengthen the heart's action, others slow it slightly and improve the blood supply. The net effect is to make a weak heart work more effectively and to reduce blood pressure. An infusion of 5gm of dried flowers and leaves per cup must be taken three times a day, long-term, to have any significant effect.

For culinary use, hawthorn berries or flowers were used to

make jellies, wines, liqueurs and sauces. For the Romans, however, the hawthorn was a symbol of hope and protection, and cuttings were brought into the home to ward off evil spirits. It also echoed the ancient British tradition that the tree was associated with marriage and fertility. Pliny wrote that: 'there are some who maintain that women who take the flower in drink conceive within 40 days'. While an old country rhyme recommends the tree as protection for man and animals in thunderstorms:

*Beware the oak — it courts the stroke.*
*Beware the ash — it courts the flash.*
*Creep under the thorn — it will save you from harm.*

Like the elder, the hawthorn was also looked upon as a doorway to Otherworld and perhaps it is this association and its links with the old pagan festivals that give the tree its 'unlucky' reputation. As is often found, there is more than a grain of truth in old wives' tales. Quite recently, it was discovered that one of the chemicals that make up the flowers' sweet scent is also produced during the decay of corpses! On the other hand, the fragrance of the blossom is also reputed to have a strong aphrodisiac effect, particularly on men. Taking all things into account, it would appear that the pre-Christian view of the hawthorn was one of protection. It is appropriate to use hawthorn for the Beltaine bonfires, which the cattle were driven through and the villagers leapt over to ensure their fertility in the coming year. Make a wish as you leap a hawthorn fire, but keep it secret to ensure that it will come true.

During May it is almost impossible to escape the scent of flowers and everywhere we can find familiar favourites — buttercups, cowslips, cow parsley and bluebells — not to mention the pink and white blossom on the apple, horse chestnut and cherry trees. Buttercups were called *ranunculus*, the Latin for 'little frog' since they were believed to grow in moist places often frequented by frogs. Despite its nursery connection of 'buttercups and daisies', the plant is poisonous and will cause blisters should the foliage remain in contact with the skin for any length of time. These inflammations can take a long time to heal and Culpeper described the plant as 'this furious biting herb'. Beggars used buttercup poultices to inflict their own skin with sores and so the plant was also known as Lararus or beggar's weed.

There are two indigenous wild cherries in Britain, the bird cherry (*prunus padus*) and the wild cherry (*prunus avium*): The wild cherry or gean, is called *idath* in Old Irish, and carries various localised names such as crab cherry, hawkberry, mazzard and merry. This is a tall, handsome tree that can grow to almost 100 feet and when it is covered with snow-white blossom in May, it is a magnificent sight, attracting swarms of butterflies and insects. The fruit of the wild cherry, as its name suggests, is black or dark red and although not as fleshy or tasty as the cultivated cherry, it is edible

Surprisingly, there are no historical or oral records of the cherry being associated with folklore in Britain although it is listed as the gum being an old remedy for coughs — hence the traditional cherry flavoured cough medicine that is still available.

Culpeper wrote that the gum dissolved in wine, 'is good for a cold, cough, and hoarseness of the throat; mendeth the colour in the face, sharpeneth the eye-sight, provoket happetite, and helpeth to break and expel the stone'. The fruit, bark and gum were all used to soothe irritating coughs, treat bronchial complaints and improve digestion. Crushed cherries, applied externally, were reputed to refresh tired skin and relieve migraines.

Modern medicine has found that certain cherries have also proved effective in treating prostate gland enlargement. Looking further a field, we find that the cherry has long been used by traditional healers from different cultures around the world. With all this information to hand, it is obvious that cherry trees have been looked upon as providing a domestic service rather than any particular magical use. In the kitchen, the fruit was cooked, eaten raw or pulped with the stones and made into wine, conserves and liqueur. Although the wild cherry listed by Aelfric is a native of Britain, it is believed that the Romans introduced the cultivated variety. Medieval herbalists grafted the more productive varieties on to the rootstock of the wild cherry and in medieval times the fruit was picked when it was wine-red, and eaten ultra-ripe.

Cherry wood (as with all the *prunus* family) gives off a wonderful perfume if the wood is burned on an open fire. If someone is cutting or pruning cherry trees, dry the wood for winter burning, or for a Beltaine fire. A cherry wand or staff would be a beautiful gift to give a woman who is a healer and/or priestess because the cherry is obviously a tree with predominantly feminine overtones. If we have to go searching for correspondences, we find that *sweet odours are also lunar, because the moon represents the physical senses and refers to the common people. Similarly, sugar and sweet things generally are much liked by children (who are classed under Luna.)*

If you can find a suitable branch for a wand or staff, a perfect libation would be cherry juice or wine.

Unlike the other species of maple, the foliage of the native field maple does not turn scarlet in autumn, but remain an attractive bright yellowish green, retaining its leaves for several weeks up to December. The leaves are much smaller than the more easily recognisable foreign species and can often be mistaken for the sycamore. The trunk is covered with pale greyish-brown bark, which in older trees is furrowed with a series of cracks; even the twigs develop ridges of gnarled bark. The field maple flowers in May or June shortly after the leaves have unfolded, producing clusters of small greenish-yellow blossoms. Like many members of the *acer* family, the field maple also produces a sweet sap in the spring that can be used for making wine or maple syrup. The brilliant autumn colours displayed by maples result from the unusually high concentration of sugar in the leaves and sap. Sugar can be extracted from the wood by boiling and Culpeper recommended decoctions of the leaves or the bark for 'strengthening the liver'.

Maple wood was highly prized and in ancient times used for making harps like those found in ancient Saxon barrows, including the Sutton Hoo burial. Using the maple for magical working is a matter for experimentation but as it is said to bring 'expansive, happy energy' to any situation it may have countless uses for a traditional witch. If we gather the glorious 'guinea-gold' coloured leaves at the Autumn Equinox, perhaps the tree could begin to play a part in a traditional Harvest Home.

There's an old country saying: that 'half the pedigree goes in at the mouth', meaning that good grazing means good livestock. During May the meadowlands are ablaze with buttercups and as soon as the clover and rye-grass have started to seed, the grass is ready for hay-making although today much of this will have already been made into silage for winter feeding. Traditionally farmers waited for a spell of good weather and worked from dawn to dusk, even taking meals out in the fields. Staying up late and enjoying the ride home on the last hay-cart as the moon came up, and a cold supper around the kitchen table, is one of those childhood memories that never fades.

This month, the whole countryside takes on a lush greenness and erupts into sound. Even if there are no mechanical noises to be heard, the sounds from the natural world can be deafening. Around the flowers, honey-bees are busy searching for nectar, their wings creating the loud hum of industry. Of the 250 different species of bee to be found in Britain, only 30 live and work together in colonies. Bees were believed to be the messengers of gods, capable of insight to a world unknown to mortal men.

Along country lanes and hedgerows cow parsley casts a delicate lace-like mist. At one time, however, it was looked upon as the Devil's Plant (as it is still called in some rural areas) because it was believed to be used by witches when casting their spells.

According to ancient texts, the classic ingredients of these 'satanic brews' were pickled cow parsley flowers and hog's dung! This is probably a later Christian overlay in an attempt to denigrate the flower which was used as part of the maidens' posies and a fertility symbol. Mixing the flowers with hog's dung was a further attempt to make the plant repulsive.

Warning: Common in England (less common elsewhere) is the hemlock, a poisonous plant much associated with witches in the past but one that appears to have a limited use in medicine. It grows mainly in damp, places but also on disturbed ground. Flowering from May to July, it grows to the height of a man and children should be warned against making blowpipes or whistles from the smooth, hollow stem. The distinguishing features are the purple blotches on the stem, its great height and attractive feathery leaves. This plant should not be confused with the innocuous cousin, cow parsley, which is much smaller and flowers from April to June.

If the month is mild, it may be possible to see another witches' familiar, the bat, flying around in the evening. If they are seen at twilight before their normal flight-times, it means that good weather is on the way. There are dozens of superstitions attached to the bat population and all of it unfounded. At one time, it was believe that if a bat flew near you, then someone was trying to betray or bewitch you, although it is generally accepted that it is unlucky to kill one.

Creatures of the shadows, bats have often been included in the ingredients of so-called witches' spells, according to Shakespeare (*Macbeth*) and Ben Jonson (*Masque of Queens*).

Because of their magical association, the bat is also looked upon as a protective charm or amulet against the powers of evil, and as a luck bringer. In the Isle of Man and parts of Wales it was believed that witches could enter a house in the form of a bat, while in Scotland if the animal was seen to fly straight up and plummet back down, it was a warning that the hour had come when witches had power over those without protective charms.

## The Hearth Fire

The fourth of May is Fairy Day. In folklore, there is a lot of mixed feeling about the Faere Folk although witches apparently have little to fear. In Welsh they are called Y Twlwyth Teg or 'The Fair People' and play such a dominant part in the folklore that they were almost seen as a parallel population right up to the introduction of popular education. Leave an offering of bread and milk on your doorstep to receive the blessings of the Faere Folk, who are strongly associated with the hawthorn. Use up stale bread and excess milk for this traditional pudding and leave a piece outside as an offering of goodwill.

## Bread and Butter Pudding

*5 oz stale bread without the crusts*
*Butter*
*2 ozs sultanas*
*Candied peel*
*2 tablespoons sugar*
*1 egg*
*½ pint milk*
*Nutmeg*

Butter a 1½ pint pie dish. Slice the bread, butter it and cut into quarters. Place half the bread in the pie dish, sprinkle on the fruit and half the sugar. Cover with remaining bread. Beat the egg and milk, pour over the bread and leave 30 minutes to soak. Sprinkle the top with remaining sugar and a little nutmeg. Bake in a moderate oven, Gas 4 (350F/180C) for about an hour.

Rich in vitamins, the countryside now offers up several 'common' weeds to add interest to our summer cooking:

**Sorrel:** Found in grassland, roadsides and woods, sorrel (*rumex acetosa*) is common throughout Britain and can easily be identified from any good book on wild flowers. As a salad, sorrel needs no dressing other than olive oil, crushed garlic and pepper.

When cooked like spinach (covered with no more water than that which remains after washing), sorrel leaves will absorb a considerable amount of butter. Nearly all the old cookery books refer to sorrel sauce — a sharp, fresh-bottled dressing made in the same way as mint sauce, by pounding the leaves and mixing them with vinegar and sugar for use throughout the year on cold meats and fish. It can also make an excellent base for vinaigrette. Grind huge quantities of sorrel with pestle and mortar, mix with white wine vinegar and a little caster sugar, then add olive oil and black pepper.

Add to mayonnaise and serve with salmon or sea-trout.

**Nettles:** These are best picked as young shoots. Both stinging nettles and white dead nettles can be harvested, washed, placed in a pan with a knob of butter and seasoning, covered and cooked until soft. Grate in nutmeg or Parmesan cheese before serving.

Nettles also make the most delicious soup. Melt onions and garlic in butter, add lots of nettles, chicken stock and a dash of wine vinegar and seasonings, liquidise and thicken as required by the addition of a boiled potato or, for a richer smoother texture, beat a little of the soup into the mixture of egg yolks and double cream. Tip this mixture into the soup and stir well over a gentle heat. Do not allow to boil.

**Lamb's Lettuce** or **Corn Salad:** The same as the version served as *mache* in expensive restaurants. This is one of the finest salads to be had and yet it can be found on arable land, hedge banks and roadsides.

**Ramsons:** Also known as wild garlic the leaves can be used to flavour salads or sauces, and make an ideal substitute for garlic or spring onions — especially with tomatoes. And as that 17th century proverbs tells us: 'Eat Leekes in Lide and ransoms in May, And all the yeare after physitians may play'.

## Weatherwise

Prolonged spells of warm weather in May are a welcome foretaste of summer, but it is dangerous to assume that winter is past and gone. Every child knows that red skies are said to be omens of forthcoming weather:

*Red sky at night, shepherd's delight,*
*Red sky in the morning, shepherd's warning.*

The omens are likely to prove correct because in Britain, with its prevailing winds from the west if, as the sun sets in the west, the air is clear of moisture, the light will take on a red hue that is reflected on the clouds in the east. That is, on those which have already passed over us and can no longer affect us. In the morning, the reverse is true, for the sun has changed its position and the light now falls on the clouds in the west, which are coming toward us. So if the red hue is seen in the morning, watch out for rain. Other countryside superstition warn:

- *Rain before seven, fine before eleven.*
- *March winds and April showers, Bring forth May flowers.*

The swallow is also a reliable weather omen. If the birds are flying high the weather will be good, but if they are seen not far from the ground then rain is on its way. A familiarity with the behaviour of local wildlife can enhance a witch's reputation.

## The Turning of the Year:

This was the old start of summer and so garlands of flowers and green leaves are part of the May celebrations, when couples can work magically together for a year of health, wealth and prosperity

> **Then**: Crops blessed.
> **Now**: The meadows are lush with new grass.

**The Circle ritual for the month should reflect thanks rather than any form of request.** It is often a positive step to go into a Circle working without being a specific reason, i.e. a request for help. The ritual should have definite feminine overtones and be one of celebration.

## Hawthorn Magic

The inhabitants of Anglo-Saxon Britain regarded the *haegthorn* as a magical plant, belonging to the woodland gods. On 1st May, the witch should visit a local sacred well or spring and cast a silver coin into the water before making a wish. Drink the water at sunrise from the horn of a cow, or wash any afflicted limbs in the water; when you leave, tie a piece of fabric or ribbon to a bush or tree nearby.

From sources like Chaucer and Shakespeare, it is known that from the medieval times it was customary for everyone, regardless of rank, to go out into the fields to *bring home the May* to decorate the houses. The foliage was collected, while the dew still remained on the leaves, by young couples who had spent the night out of doors; garlands of green boughs were then brought home to bring good luck. This custom continued well into the

Elizabethan era. Hawthorn bushes growing on top of mounds (i.e. Glastonbury) were thought to be entrances to the Otherworld and connected to the Faere Folk.

Other claims for the tree are:
- Eat three hawthorn leaves to aid meditation at a sacred spot.
- Hawthorn charcoal can produce heat that would melt pig iron.
- Thread berries on a cord to use as a Witches' Ladder.
- Carry a thorn from the tree in a pouch to bring luck when fishing.
- Medieval texts claim that witches turned into hawthorn trees.
- Eat young shoots and flowers in a sandwich as 'bread and cheese'.

The tree can be used to protect babies and young children by hanging a sprig above a child's bed to bring them under the protection of the goddess/guardian, or keep a pouch of the leaves sewn into the pillow. Hawthorn can also be planted by the home to keep out evil or negative influences and protect it from lightning strikes; it was also said that cattle thrived in fields where hawthorn grew.

- Make a wash of flowers and leaves to sprinkle around the house to repel evil spirits and negative energies.
- The wood, berries and leaves can also be burnt in incense form to purify and attract beneficent energies.
- An infusion of berries (known as haws or hags) gives added protection when dispelling negative energies.
- In times of trouble or depression take an infusion of the flowers or leaves, or burn them as incense.

The flowering tops and berries all have similar properties and are used to improve the blood supply and reduce blood pressure. It is a good tonic to take daily for anyone in middle age, especially where there is a history of heart disease in the family. For a daily infusion take one teaspoon of flowers and leaves and seep in boiling water for five minutes. Keep them covered to retain maximum benefit during the infusion. The flowers and leaves can be gathered and dried for use out of season.

### The Witch's 'Midsummer Men'

*I remember the mayds (especially the cooke-mayds and dairy-mayds) would stick up in some chinkes of the joists Midsomer-men, which are slips of orpins: they placed them by paires, sc. one for such a man the other for such a mayd his sweetheart, and accordingly as the orpin did incline to, or recline from the other; that there would be love, or aversion; if either did wither death.* Orpine (*sedum telephium*) is particularly suited to this type of use as it remains fresh long after being gathered. Not only can it be used as an attraction-spell but also by using reverse psychology, the spell can become a curse to drive a couple apart.

Chapter Eight

# June — Flower Moon

June can also be called the Flower or Honey Moon as a time for celebration — represented by the Oak, symbol of the god in his guise as Oak King, or the Green Man. The oak is the king of the woodland, especially if bearing mistletoe. The oak is also one of the Seven Chieftain Trees (named in old Irish law; the felling of any oak was considered a serious crime). The other six were the hazel, apple, yew, holly, ash and pine. Celtic names for June contain the words of 'mid' or 'middle', as this month was regarded by the Celts as the height of summer. In Welsh it is *Mehefin*, in Irish-Gaelic *Meitheamb*, and in Scottish-Gaelic *Meadhan-Samhraidh*. The Anglo-Saxons called it 'Mow-month' or *Weyd-monath* — *'because the beats did then weyd in the meadow, that is to say, go and feed there'*. In the 14th century misericord calendar, it was shown as the time for hawking and leisure. The Summer Solstice falls on or around the 21st.

June is generally regarded as the first month of summer when the hours of daylight are at their longest; in northernmost parts of Europe, there is very little darkness in the latter half of the month around the time of the Solstice. For our agricultural ancestors, there were only two seasons: summer and winter. Summer was welcomed in with merriment and pageantry as part of its May Day rituals, while the solstice on the 21st June marked the turning point of the year, as the sun began its slow descent into winter.

Those far-off midsummer ceremonies involved the lighting of bonfires on hilltops and village greens, around which the local populace would gather. Cattle were driven through the flames to cure any sick animals, and to guard against harm of any kind in the coming year. Young men and girls would jump over the flames to ensure a good harvest and the parents of the young people who bounded the highest over the fire would have the most abundant crop.

The sun was ritually strengthened by bonfires burning everywhere on Midsummer Eve; with torch-lit processions through the streets of the towns, and straw-bound wheels set alight and rolled down steep rural hillsides into the valleys below. By the Middle Ages this was said to be in homage to St John but these midsummer celebrations were considerably older, dating back to pre-Christian times. The bonfires also drove out evil (ill luck) and brought the promise of fertility and prosperity to men, crops and livestock. Lit on the windward side of the fields, the life-giving smoke blew over the crops, while blazing gorse was carried around penned animals to protect them from disease or accident.

Another much later fire custom involved the belief in a magical coal that should be taken 'live' from the hearth on Midsummer's Day between 10 and 12 noon, and buried in the garden without the person concerned speaking to anyone, to bring luck to the household in the coming year. The luck could also be transferred to anyone finding a piece of buried coal on Midsummer's Day, although the power of the charm varied, as did the plant under which it could be found. A coal discovered under the root of mugwort, for example, would keep the finder safe from plague, carbuncle, lightning, quartain ague and from burning. A piece found under the root of plantain should be placed under the pillow that night, in order to discover the identity of a future husband in a dream.

After the June summer showers, Nature is at her most beautiful. Elder blooms in the hedgerows, while clover, bird's-foot trefoil, yellow flags, comfrey and forget-me-nots add a riot of colour to meadows, downlands and stream banks. The country name for the wild honeysuckle is woodbine; 'honeysuckle' refers to the sweet nectar of the flowers. Although the berries are extremely poisonous, the plant was used for treating colds, asthma, constipation, skin infections and urinary complaints. Since the Middle Ages, honeysuckle has been a symbol of fidelity and affection and walking along any country lane towards dusk, you will be overwhelmed by the perfume of the honeysuckle — which will often flower again in September.

Beware, however, of the dwarf elder (also known as danewort) that is said to grow wherever the blood of Danes was spilt, and although it is closely related to the common elder, its berries have a strong purgative effect and are slightly poisonous. In midsummer (a little later than the common elder), it produces large flat clusters of white or pink flowers with purple, vanilla-scented anthers. It is usually found growing in hedgerows, churchyards and near old ruins.

During medieval times, clover was grown as a forage crop, or ploughed back into the ground to enrich the soil. The flowers were (and still are) valued by bee-keepers, because the nectar from clover makes superior honey. The plant was used medicinally to treat a variety of complaints with Culpeper writing that made into an ointment it 'is good to apply to the bites of venomous creatures'. Birds-foot trefoil is better known as 'bacon and eggs' because of the red and orange of the flowers. About seventy local names have been recorded for the plant and several species were used medici-nally during the Middle Ages. This is one of the commonest members of the pea family, which helps to enrich the soil and is often grown alongside clover for this purpose.

The yellow flag blooms at the water's edge, a magnificent golden *fleur-de-lys* among sword-shaped leaves. Despite the fact that the root and leaves of the flag, or wild iris, are poisonous, it has been used in the past in many herbal remedies. The roots contain orris which, when powdered, was used for medicinal purposes. The true forget-me-not is also to be found growing in profusion among brackish waterside vegetation of stream banks and ditches, where it forms into dense beds of striking blue flowers. In the years following the Battle of Waterloo, the flowers sprang up all over the battlefield as a result of the disturbed soil — the same conditions that produced the famous poppy-fields of Flanders after the First World War.

Comfrey blooms from mid-May to early July, the tall stems overhanging stream and riverbanks. The plant has bell-shaped flowers that vary greatly in colour from reddish-purple and dull violet to creamy-yellow, dirty white, or a mixture of all four.

Comfrey had (and still has) numerous uses, especially when used for healing bruises, wounds and sprains. The leaves also make an excellent compost and mulch, and no witch worth her salt is without a clump of this plant in her garden — even if only the miniature variety. Preparations made from the roots and leaves were once used to treat sores, wounds and various ailments.

Herb Robert is connected with 'Robin Goodfellow' and other 'Robin' names that have links with the Faere Folk. The plant grows in a variety of places from damp woods, hedgerows, among rocks and on seashore shingle. It is recognised by its pink flowers and fern-like divided leaves, often tinged with red. It flowers throughout the summer, the pink blossoms dropping downwards at night or in bad weather. It also has a wide range of medicinal uses.

The hedgerows also abound with over 100 species of wild rose, the most familiar being the dog rose (*rosa canina*) with its delicate shell-pink flowers. The fruits of wild roses are rich in Vitamin C and during the WWII a campaign to collect them each autumn produced 2 ½ million bottles of rose-hip syrup, which contained as much Vitamin C as 25 million oranges! Recent research has also revealed that rosehip is more effective than glucosamine for easing the symptoms of arthritis suffers.

The dark green leaves of the elder (see **November**) keep flies at bay; in the past, they were dried and used as an insecticide, so a sprig of elder hanging up in the house or worn on a hat will send flies packing. Elder leaves also make a useful ointment for bruises, sprains and wounds. An elder tree in flower is a magnificent sight with its enormous heads of creamy white blossoms and a heady fragrance and while the flowers can be used to make elderflower champagne, they are also useful in raising the resistance to respiratory infections. An ointment made from elder flowers is excellent for chilblains and stimulating local circulation, not to mention popular hay fever treatments for their anti-catarrhal properties.

The berries are small and green at first, ripening to deep purple clusters that weigh down the branches. These are made into wine, chutney, jellies and ketchup. Medicinally, both the berries and the flowers encourage fever response and stimulate sweating, which prevents very high temperatures and provides an important channel for detoxification. To cure warts, rub them with a green elder twig, which should then be buried. As the wood rots so will the wart disappear. It is quite surprising with all its beneficial properties that the elder gets such a bad press to connect it with all manner of devils, demons and bad 'uns.

Fairy rings are circles of rank or withered grass, often seen in meadows. These were said to be produced by the Faere Folk dancing on the spot. In sober truth, these rings are simply an agaric or fungus below the surface, which has seeded in a circular pattern, as many plants do. Where the ring is brown and almost bare, the 'spawn' is of a greyish-white colour; the grass dies because the spawn envelopes the roots to prevent their absorbing moisture. Where the grass is rank, the 'spawn' is dead, and serves as manure to the young grass. For good luck, leave a small token inside the ring, saying:

*You demi-puppets, that*
*By moonshine do the green-sour ringlets make ....*
Shakespeare: The Tempest, v.1

June is the time to learn about the vocal abilities of the various species of wild life. Alarm calls of birds protecting young can be almost deafening but it allows for easier identification when we can see who is making all the noise. The hysterical screech of the blackbird, or the frantic chipping of the wren will soon tell us if there is a cat or crow about. Grey squirrels also have a remarkable repertoire for communicating danger, or seeing off a rival.

Found along the waterside are the oldest of all insects — the dragonfly. Fossilised remains found in coal strata reveal that enormous dragonflies with a wingspan of more than 27 inches patrolled the prehistoric swamps of the Carboniferous Period. Although this amazing creature rarely lives for more than a month, it can reach speeds of up to 50-60 miles an hour and can detect prey at a distance of 40 yards away. Despite appearances, its large gauzy wings are colourless. They glisten in the sun and this effect harmonises with the insect's brightly coloured body to produce those brilliant flashes of green, blue and gold. In folklore the dragonfly was referred to as the 'sewing needle', or 'devil's darning needle', because it was believed to be able to fly into a person's ear and sew it up! It was thought to be in league with adders and warn them of approaching danger.

## The Hearth Fire:

The 20th June is the Feast of Cerridwen, celebrated at the turning of the year. Burn vervain incense for her and prepare a supper of roast pork. As an alternative, try a traditional Welsh *cawl* or leek broth. Early Welsh manuscripts tell us that this would be made when a piece of bacon was being boiled and would either be served as a first course, or kept for another meal. The ingredients were governed by what vegetables were to hand or in season.

## Cawl Cennin

*1½ pints bacon stock*
*8 oz potatoes, peeled and diced*
*8 oz carrots, diced*
*2 leeks, sliced*
*½ small cabbage, shredded*
*2 tablespoons oatmeal (optional)*
*Salt and pepper*
*Chopped parsley*

Put the potatoes and carrots in the stock, bring to the boil and cook for 10 minutes. Add the leeks and cabbage. Mix oatmeal with a little cold water and add. Bring to the boil again and simmer for 10 to 15 minutes until the vegetables are cooked. Check for seasoning. Serve sprinkled with chopped parsley.

Wild food is increasingly abundant with Nature's luxuries beginning to appear — elderflowers for a delicious sparkling wine; wild strawberries best eaten straight from the plant; or fresh petals of the dog-rose added to a salad.

## Sparkling Elder Flower Champagne

*7 pints water*
*1½ lbs sugar*
*8 elder flower heads*
*1 sliced orange*
*1 sliced lemon*
*2 tablespoons white wine vinegar*

Boil the water, pour over the sugar in a large container and cover with a clean cloth. When cold add the flowers, orange, lemon and vinegar, cover and leave for 24 hours. Strain, squeezing the flowers to extract all the juice. Bottle in glass bottles, seal well and set aside for two weeks before drinking. Serve as a refreshing drink for summer evenings and especially a Midsummer ritual.

Elderflowers can be eaten straight off the branch and, according to Richard Mabey in *Food For Free,* on a hot summer's day the taste is 'as frothy as a glass of ice-cream soda'.

## Weatherwise

Warm dry weather in June is ideal but crops need rain for growth, as well as sun for ripening and this month sees the start of the season for summer storms. In British country-lore the oak tree has long has the reputation of being a safe place to shelter during a thunderstorm although there is the popular rhyme that disagrees: *Beware of the oak; it draws the stroke.* Oak trees were believed to be the home of the gods of lightening because they always appeared to attract the flash. The acorn shapes that are used as blind-pulls were also thought to protect the house from lightning strikes. There is a lot of superstition surrounding storms and today people will still cover mirrors and hide all metal objects during a thunderstorm. In some areas the front and back doors will be left open so that if the lightning gets in, it can get out again without causing any damage.

Even more spectacular at this time of year is the night storm heralded by the still, sultry atmosphere and desultory breeze that warns of the storm's approach. The temperature drops and the wind increases, as large spots of rain begin to fall. The sky darkens to provide the backdrop for an impressive display of both sheet and forked lightning. These early summer storms are usually briefer than those in July and August, with the prolonged rainfall (with or without thunder) reaching maximum frequency during August, when the witch will draw on all that free natural energy to power magical workings!

- June damp and warn does the farmer no harm
- A cold and wet June spoils the rest of the year

In Britain, any of these combinations is possible, but typical June weather is generally perceived as being pleasant, with the sun at its hottest around the time of the Solstice.

Summer also provides us with some spectacular sunrises and sunsets. When there is high atmospheric pressure there are often large amounts of high-level cirriform cloud (from the Latin *cirrus* — meaning a hair-like tuft) composed of ice-crystals.

Around sunrise and sunset, when the sun's rays pass obliquely through the atmosphere, the sunlight is broken up in such a manner that the colours at the blue end of the spectrum 'disappear' behind the yellows and reds. This occurs more often when the air is dry and hazy. These colours, combined with the light and shadow of the clouds, create a wider range of light from gold to crimson — even purple. A green sky above the sunset, however, foretells rain the next day. While *Mare's tails and mackerel sky; not long wet and not long dry*, refers to the patterns of the high clouds and indicates showery weather.

Sudden squalls of rain can often produce what country people call a 'fox's wedding' — when a sudden splatter of raindrops while the sun is shining, produces a glorious rainbow. There is an older belief that the rainbow is a soul-bridge and many people still wish when they see one, especially if it is a double (i.e. reflected) bow. Used as a weather omen, if a rainbow is seen in the morning then there is rain to come; if it appears in the afternoon, the next day will be fine.

Although daisies and dandelions are not popular with gardeners, both are actually good weather omens, for when the petals are seen to be closing then bad weather is on the way. Robins are also good for weather warnings. If the bird is sheltering in the branches of a tree or hedge then rain is on the way. If the bird sits high on an open branch or on telegraph wires fine weather is imminent. This kind of weather-lore is not necessarily superstitious nonsense since there is always a good reason why birds, animals and plants react the way they do under certain weather conditions.

Scientists dismiss the idea of plants and animals making 'long-term predictions about the weather' but most country people are interested in the short-term. Natural weather forecasting is natural to the witch and countryman. Both know that many different types of flower close their petals before rain, why cows lie down and swifts disappear. This is because flora and fauna are much better at detecting barometric pressure than man. The flowers detect increased humidity, for example, while the cows are probably picking up on a change in air pressure, and settling down in a dry spot prior to a deluge.

Likewise, swallows traditionally hunt low in bad weather but high in fine. On a hot day, tiny meadowland insects are lifted higher into the air by the convection currents rising from the warm fields, while on cooler days they will be lower down.

Similarly, swifts spend almost their entire lives on the wing and cannot sit out bad weather. Instead, they fly over or around an approaching front, abandoning their nests for up to three days. Meanwhile, their young go into a form of suspended animation, slowing down their energy requirements until the parents return. Bees are just as uncomfortable flying in the rain, but they return to the shelter of the hive before a downpour. Again, they are probably picking up minute changes in barometric pressure but the witch can always make use of these behaviour patterns.

## The Turning of the Year

The Summer Solstice falls on the 21st — which was old Midsummer's Day. The church altered this to 24th to coincide with the Feast of St John. In Celtic times, great bonfires were lit to honour the sun god and on the following morning, village folk and livestock were passed over the burning embers to ward of disease and ill luck. It was a last opportunity for leisure before the start of the harvest.

**Then:** Hawking scene.

**Now:** Ears of corn begin to appear and trees are in full leaf.

**The Circle ritual for this month should reflect the masculine principles of magical working and be accompanied by a mini-bonfire made of oak twigs.** For the traditional witch this is an important and powerful time for Craft working, even although it is generally observed by modern paganism as a 'minor sabbat'.

## Oak Magic

The old saying: 'two hundred years growing, two hundred years staying, and two hundred years dying', reflects the great age, which oaks can achieve. Much of European folklore is based upon an inherent reverence for the oak, whose human qualities included a voice that screamed and groaned in agony if the tree was felled — *as if it were the genius of the oake lamenting*. Touching wood for luck is an expression of these ancient beliefs, reflecting the respect given to the guardian spirits of the tree. The close grain of oak means that the wood burns slowly and gives off a lot of heat; although magical need-fires should not be fuelled with oak timber, the fire can be lit with a brand of burning oak.

It has also been suggested that the name of the Celtic priesthood — the Druids — came from the root-word for the oak, *duir*, as both mean 'tree', or more specifically 'oak tree'. The oak was also the emblem of the Black Prince (Edward, Prince of Wales and son of Edward III), who wore a coronet of oak leaves over his helmet.

Pagan marriages were sometimes conducted beneath solitary oak trees, which later became identified as Marriage Oaks.Throughout our island history, oaks have been seen as having strong protective auras that can be used to boost personal physical or magical strength. Place your hands flat against the trunk and you may be able to feel the energies of the tree in the form of a tingling sensation. If you return to the same tree several times and repeat the exercise, you will find that the responses become stronger. The bulk of oak-lore that has been passed down has been in the form of charms for romance, but if we learn to look *behind* the coy Victorian overlay of these 'superstitions', it is possible to use oak magic for much more than trivial love spells and re-connect with the Old Ways.

## Chapter Nine

# The Witch's Hedgerow

Gaining more sunlight than the woodland, yet more sheltered than the open field, the spring hedgerow supports a wide selection of early flowers. From the dry bank top to the damp ditch, each has its own special habitat and by early summer, the strongest growth begins to dominate. With the profusion of blossom come the insects, also more abundant here than in the woods. As summer progresses the ground plants grow to the height of the hedge, tangling with the fresh shoots of the shrub layer. The spring flowers evolve into fruits and seeds, while birds adapt their feeding habits accordingly.

By autumn, climbing plants like bittersweet and the black and white bryonies reach the top of the hedge. Ferns dominate the hedge bottom with bracken growing to its full height of up to seven feet or more; the dampness of the hedge bank by the ditch suits smaller ferns such as the harts tongue. The main winter activity of the hedgerow takes place beneath the accumulated litter of fallen leaves and dying vegetation at the foot of the hedge and in the soil itself, the comparative warmth and shelter of the hedge attracting insects from the open fields.

In 2004, hedge-cutting was banned between March and July to protect nesting birds, and there must also be a six-foot protection zone along hedges, ditches and watercourses, which must be unsprayed, unfertilised and uncultivated … which is where the witch will find her magical ingredients. There are now only 500,000 miles of hedgerows left in England, and unfortunately very little of it has been traditionally maintained. Only the hands and eye of a skilled craftsman 'wielding that ancient tool the billhook, with the wrist-power of a blacksmith, and the finesse of a snooker champion' can achieve the compact, intertwining that no bullock can break through.

This artistry was reserved for the winter months: the weather might be too bad for working in the fields but the hedgerow had to be maintained. The survival of the hedge is vital to the countryside because:

- Hedges are important for wildlife — and so are the corners of the fields where the plough or mower cannot reach; a tangle of scrub creates triangular patches of uncultivated ground and here the ubiquitous bramble grows the thickest.

- Hedges are important for livestock. Cattle lying down in the lee of a hedge are a sign of bad weather to come; hedges warm the fields for animals turned out in them. Stand downwind behind a hedge, and even when it is leafless the air is still, and it feels warm. The windbreak effect of a hedge under normal weather conditions extends over the adjacent 50-70 yard strip of pasture. In hard weather, that is where the beasts gather: they know.

- Hedges are important for witches. This is a storehouse of raw ingredients for spells and healing; and the place to encounter the birds and animals useful for divination. Its flowers and herbs offer remedies against present ills and charms against those to come.

As any traditional witch will know, hawthorn is the most common tree to be found in the hedgerow, although many include blackthorn and holly. Other species arrive as seeds — dog rose and ash soon appear while others, like hazel and field maple are slow to colonise. A hedge planted as pure hawthorn slowly acquires additional species as it gets older and scientific studies of the 'species diversity' of hedgerows in relation to their age (where this can be reasonably accurately dated from historical records), have suggested that there is more or less a direct relationship between the number of species established in a hedge and its age.

There is a long-held belief in botanical circles that each 30-yard section of hedge gains a new species every century, but now landscape archaeologists are disputing this. Richard Muir writing in *Ancient Trees: Living Landscapes* points out that even a basic knowledge of ecology reveals that a species that is singularly well adjusted to its environment will flourish and expand at the expense of less well-adjusted neighbours. Obviously, this is as true in a hedgerow as it is in a thicket, or on a railway embankment.

If a shrub is 'happy' in a hedge then, over time it can be expected to spread, displacing competing species that are less 'at home' there. In this way, a species-rich hedgerow becomes not richer but *poorer* in species. For example, holly can be seen to self-layer, which explains many of the long stretches in northern hedges that are monopolised by holly. Blackthorn can also spread aggressively, as can be seen along the Roman roads including the Via Devana in southern England, where blackthorn has advanced from and along roadside hedges to form a dense tunnel shading the route.

Hedgerows associated with Saxon boundaries are often invoked in hedge-dating literature. Yet sometimes the course of their boundaries is uncertain and the boundary mentioned might have been Roman, or even prehistoric. After all, we know of a few extant boundary hedges that existed in Saxon times, so a hedge mentioned by the Saxons might well have been of Iron Age, or even of Bronze Age origin! A witch lucky enough to tread *these* boundaries will be following in the ancestral footsteps of countless generations of cunning men and women.

Another familiar sight are the old pollards — trees that have been cut to produce successive crops of wood at a height of 6 – 15 feet above the ground so that grazing animals cannot reach the young shoots. Pollarding was carried out on wood-pasture and hedgerows rather than in the woods, although from a historical perspective, pollarding allowed livestock to graze common land of the parish, which often included some woodland. As a result, this type of wood-pasture developed its own appearance. It has a bare grassy floor (for the animals destroyed the spring flowers and undergrowth) and the trees were well spaced because the animals also ate many of the new saplings. Supplies of poles were obtained by cropping the branches of the trees at head height and this became known as 'pollarding' from the word mean 'head'.

Old pollards can still be seen today and although the technique has all but died out, it has been well documented since Anglo-Saxon times. Apart from wood-pasture, many old pollards can be found in hedges, in farmland as boundary markers, or along water-courses. This is the ideal source for obtaining a witch's magical tool from one of these old trees, because willow is one of the woods from which to make a traditional magic wand or staff. This should be cut from the tree with a single blow, having first asked the tree for its permission and a suitable offering having been made. Shaman, sorcerers and enchanters were all said to favour wands made of willow because it can be used to command the spirits of the dead.

These magical associations were obviously well known, as existing folklore claims that using a willow staff to herd animals is guaranteed to drive them to the 'devil'; and that using a willow wand to renounce your baptism was said to guarantee the devil would grant you supernatural powers. These beliefs are, no doubt, throwbacks to pre-Christian times when willow was acknowledged as being the 'badge' of the cunning man or woman.

**Meditation Exercise**

Meditation is the contemplation of the inner recesses of the mind on a *spiritual theme*, often used to 'receive' solutions to problematic situations in the mundane world, or to point the way in spiritual matters. Here we need to focus on an item or image that we find relaxing such as:

- Drifting clouds
- The sound of a rippling stream or fountain
- The breeze rustling in the leaves
- Birdsong

If we are unable to get out into the countryside we can still focus on drifting clouds, even if it only happens to be looking out of a window. Playing specially recorded CDs aimed at creating a relaxing atmosphere can easily reproduce the 'sounds'.

By sitting quietly and clearing the mind of all extraneous thought, we concentrate on — nothing. We focus on the form of a slow moving, snowy-white cloud against a deep blue sky and close our mind to everything else. Or we close our eyes and concentrate on the gentle sound of falling water, birdsong or the wind rustling among the leaves of the trees.

If nothing else, we will find the exercise relaxes the mind, body and spirit. With constant use, however, we will quickly find that when our mind becomes a blank canvass, we become more receptive to the creative thoughts and impulses that can often solve those problematic situations that cause us stress and worry.

## The Witch's Recharging Spell

*An old lady living near to me was conversing with a neighbour during a summer storm and remarked that there was nothing to cause alarm, as sheet lightening was just sent to ripen the corn.* Harnessing this kind of magical energy means acting spontaneously whenever a storm is in the offing. If you have a recently set a spell that could benefit from being recharged by natural elements, expose the bottle, bag or image to the electrical energies with the request that the charm be 'hastened to fruition just like the ripening corn'.

Chapter Ten

# July — Lightning Moon

**July was known as the Lightning Moon because of the particular violence of summer storms -— represented by the Birch. In many parts of the country the birch is also associated with May Eve celebrations when people used to go out overnight into the woods and bring home green boughs to decorate their homes for May Day. It is a tree of good luck and purification,and because it is used in the making of the besom, it is considered to be a feminine symbol; it is also referred to as *the lady of the woods*. For the Anglo-Saxons it was *Maedmonath* from the *meads* or meadows being in bloom. In the 14th century misericord calendar, it was shown as the time for baking the loaves for Lammas.**

The patchwork landscape of the countryside is transformed this month, as crops ripen and fields turn from green to gold. There is little respite between haymaking and the beginning of the harvest, and it was considered unlucky (or simply inconvenient) to marry at this time: *They that wive 'twixt sickle and scythe shall never thrive.*

Perhaps the most evocative **sound** of an English summer, however, is the drone of the bumblebee as it flies low over the ground in its own peculiar zigzagging search for nectar. In reality, the first bumblebees (usually a queen) can be seen as early as February or March when they emerge from hibernation to seek out a new nesting site, although the colony only survives one year. And if there are clear **visions** to epitomise an English summer it would probably be a buttercup meadow gleaming gold in the sun, or a slow moving river overhung with willow trees

Of the days when every lowland village had its basket maker and its 'withy' beds, Richard Jefferies wrote:

> An advantage of willow is that it enables the farmer to derive a profit from land that would otherwise be comparatively valueless, to provide arable farms with market baskets, chaff baskets, bassinets and hampers. This willow harvest is looked forward to by the cottagers who live along the rivers as an opportunity for earning extra money.

Today the willow is popularly used to make biodegradable coffins for pagan and woodlands burials.

All willows (see **April**) belong to the large family of *Salix*, which has between 350 and 500 species, depending on the source you consult. This confusion arises because hybrids occur together with parent species and because the willows themselves are variable. Medicinally, the bark of the white willow was used to alleviate pain, relieve headaches, and reduce fevers. It was also used for rheumatism, arthritis, internal bleeding, inflammations, gout, heartburn, colds, nervous insomnia, digestive problems and stomach complains. Externally, it was applied for burns, sores, cuts and skin rashes. Culpeper wrote: 'The leaves are bruised and boiled in wine, and drank, stays the heat of lust in man or woman, and quite distinguishes it, if it be long used.'

It wasn't so long ago that common wild plants were widely used for their medicinal properties but it is possible that in the not too distant future EU directives will make it uneconomic for herbalists to supply natural remedies. So collecting wild plants and making potions will be the only way we can access traditional medicines, many of which go back to medieval times. They have a very long history …

The local wise-woman would have used dried reeds and rushes to strew across the floor of her cottage — something we often imitate by having woven fibre mats to make a stone kitchen floor a little more welcoming. The scent of meadowsweet, or 'queen of the meadows' was the reason why the plant was collected by medieval housewives and strewn among the rushes. The Druids, however, prized meadowsweet as one of their Three Sacred Herbs, in addition to vervain and watermint.

Mugwort has various magical properties attributed to it and was believed to be a protection against thunder, offset traveller's fatigue and reveal evil influences. It was used in traditional recipes for stuffing geese, port, duck and game; and medicinally for depression and loss of appetite. While white dead nettle provided a soothing and astringent tea from the leaves that helped with cystitis and other female complaints.

The ox-eye daisy was good for chesty coughs: 'The daisies do mitigate all kinde of paines, but especially in the joints, and gout, if they be stamped with new butter unsalted, and applied upon the pained place ...' (*The Herball, or Generall Historie of Plantes,* 1597). Common plantain is a soothing, anti-histamine and anti-allergenic; tea mad from leaves soothes the stomach; crushed stem and leaves make a good poultice for cuts. Self-heal was widely used to stop bleeding or its crushed leaves used in a poultice. It lowers fever and blood pressure.

Herb Robert was used for wound healing, while tea from the leaves can help sooth mouth ulcers; the leaves can also be crushed and used as a poultice. Like Herb Robert and all members of the cranesbill family, hedgerow cranesbill also has excellent wound-healing properties.

Agrimony blooms during the summer and autumn on hedge-banks and roadsides. Also called *lemmade* or bunch-flower, its apricot scented foliage is used by herbalists to make tea and medicine to treat liver complaints. The whole plant contains tannin, which produces a yellow dye for textiles.

In the Middle Ages St John's Wort was known as *fuga Daemonum – the blessed herb which protects the common folk from horrible charms.* Evil it was claimed, took flight at the mere whiff of its scent. It was used as a major wound healer, particularly for deep sword wounds. Today used externally the oil's healing and mild analgesic properties help to ease the pain caused by arthritis, neuralgia, burns and wounds. To make the infused oil, collect the flowers in June or July and pack them into a jar containing sunflower oil. Leave on a sunny window sill for at least a fortnight and then press out and filter the oil, which will have turned a deep red colour because of the hypericin in it.

The ancient name for foxgloves, *foxes glofa*, allegedly refers to the belief that witches placed the blooms over the feet of foxes to enable them to perform their mischief in silence. Other sources suggest that the flower was named after a 12th century musical instrument that was a collection of small bells hung upon a thin leather strap. Wild foxgloves are a magnificent sight in summer where they can be found on sunny woodland slopes and in lush shadowed groves, the leaves are, however, deadly. From earliest times the plant has been used by herbalists and known as a symbol of both poisoning and healing — in later times the extracted digitalis was found to be extremely useful in treating heart conditions.

**Warning: the use of St John's Wort externally can trigger sun-sensitive skin rashes. If this occurs, stop applying the oil and avoid exposure to sunlight.**

July marks the height of summer and the beginning of the Dog Days (3rd), marked by the ascendance of Sirius in the southern hemisphere. 'In these Dog Days it is forbidden by Astronomy to all Manner of People to be let Blood or take Physic. Yea, it is good to abstain all this time from Women.' (*The Husbandman's Journal*).

For the traditional witch, our Dog Days are heralded by the blooming of the dog-rose. The wild dog rose, eglantine or briar is the emblem of England, and by July reigns as queen of the hedgerows with its shell-pink colouring of the delicate petals that make other flowers seem gaudy by comparison. From the plant comes a faint, lingering fragrance on the early morning breeze, and in country areas the briar was traditionally planted on the graves of lost sweethearts and lovers.

Shakespeare expressed his admiration for the *faire eglantine*: 'I had rather be a canker [dog rose] in a hedge than a rose in all his grace.' In medieval times the leaves were used as a mild laxative and, being astringent, for healing wounds. Rose water made a soothing antiseptic tonic for sore and sensitive skin. The petals of roses have antispasmodic, sedative and astringent properties being locally antiseptic and a gentle laxative. Rosewater is a gentle skin cleanser. Because of the laws governing the picking of wild flowers, cultivated rose petals may be used instead of wild briar.

**For the best results use fresh petals for an infusion:**
*1 grm petals per cup.*

At first glance the briar and bramble thicket appears like an impenetrable tangle of vicious tentacles but the witch knows that this is colonised by an enormous range of wild animals, birds and insects that find food, shelter and safety among the thorny, arching branches. Through the summer months, the five-petalled white or pink bramble blossoms cover the bushes. The flowering season is lengthy and blackberries develop from late August to October, which means that the bushes can produce flowers, unripe green berries, half-ripe red ones and fully ripe black-berries, at the same time.

Bramble leaves were also used as an astringent and tonic; and as a poultice to treat burns, swellings and ulcers. Externally they were used as a mouthwash, or as a gargle for sore throats and gum inflammations. Bleeding caused by the thorns while black-berry picking can be stemmed by rubbing the freshly cut leaves on the scratches.

Most people are affected by thunderstorms — some (and

witches in particular) find them exhilarating, while others cower under the stairs at the first distant rumble of thunder. An approaching storm can cause headaches in humans and restless behaviour in animals and birds, which may explain why in folklore storms have always been regarded as something more than natural phenomena. In almost every ancient culture, storms have been seen as a manifestation of the gods. This is not surprising since a typical discharge of lightning contains the equivalent of 1,000 volts of electricity and a build-up of heat to more than 10,000C (or 20,000F). The heated air expands and this is heard as thunder.

Because of the different speeds of light and sound, a roll or clap of thunder is always heard after the lightning. Sound takes about five seconds to travel a mile through the air but if the lightning strike is close, the thunder will be heard as a deafening bang, a fraction of a second after the flash. Forked lightning travelling from cloud to ground is often a mile long, while cloud-to-cloud flashes may extend over several miles. No matter how fascinating the storm, it is unwise to stand outside in the open or shelter under a tree, as you could find yourself acting as a conductor!

Church bells were often rung during storms because they were believed to have power over the evil forces causing the disturbance. For this reason, the legend *Fulgura Frango* was often inscribed on those dating back to medieval times. An 8th century formula for the blessing of church bells says: 'Whenever this bell sounds, let the power of enemies retire. So also the shadow of phantoms, the assault of whirlwinds, the stroke of lightnings, the injury of tempests and every spirit of the storm winds.'

Although the sound of church bells on a summer's evening stirs pleasant memories of rural England, bell ringing was a method of communicating news of a death to the community. It was three-times-three for a man and three-times-two for a woman, followed by the number of years they'd lived. If the tolling bell sounded the three-score-years-and-ten the deceased was thought to have had a 'good innings' but if the bell stopped after a low number a hush would come over the fields.

It was generally accepted that until the 'passing bell' had been rung the soul remained earth-bound as it only 'rose to heaven on the sound of the bell'. This practice was stopped at the onset of WWII, when all the bells of England were silenced and it has never been revived. Another country funeral practice that has survived is informing the bees of a death in the family. Following a death, the widow or eldest surviving child had to go and tell the bees. Some said if you didn't, the bees would die or leave. A witch will understand the importance of this simple rite and should make a point of communicating any household news to the colony, even if it's only the wild bees in the old stone wall.

## The Hearth Fire

Coming in from the July fields, having watched the stars appearing one by one against the night sky, it is pleasant to sit and relax with a simple meal at the kitchen table, while the night noises come in through the open doors and windows. An ideal summer supper, served with salad picked fresh from the garden would be:

### Farmhouse Scramble

*3 eggs*
*3 oz cooked ham*
*Mustard to taste*
*1/2 gill milk*
*1 oz butter*
*6 oz cooked potatoes*
*1 tblsp chopped jack by the hedge*

Beat the eggs in a basin. Add milk. Rub potatoes through a fine sieve and stir into the beaten egg mix. Add the ham, finely minced, jack by the hedge, and the mustard to taste. Melt butter in a frying pan. Pour in the mixture. As it begins to set, let the liquid run below the edges and cook till the whole is set.

By the calendar reckoning 31st July is Lughnasadh Eve, or the festival of the corn harvest, but by lunar reckoning it should be left a fortnight until the more appropriate Harvest Moon. This is the traditional start of autumn when everyone would be working late out in the fields in order to gather in the harvest. There would be six weeks of intense labour and in the kitchen, there would be plenty going on in terms of homemade wine, bottled fruit, pickles and jams for the coming winter. Try this traditional recipe:

## Mead
*4 lbs honey*
*1 gallon spring water*
*1 each large orange and lemon*
*1 cup grape juice*
*A little yeast*

Boil water and honey till dissolved. Cool, add lemon and orange juice with rinds finely grated. Add yeast and stir well. Pour into a barrel and stop up. Place in a dark cupboard somewhere warm. Let air out occasionally but leave three months to work. Take off clear liquid and bottle. Ready in one week, but better if left a year.

When it comes to wild food, the wise witch will have earmarked the best, south-facing trees and bushes for the earliest crops. In addition to enjoying the indescribable taste of freshly picked fruits, there is plenty of time to turn the excess into jams, jellies and pickles for the winter.

## Weatherwise

Although July is one of the hottest months of the year, weather lore seems to be preoccupied with rain:

> *If the first day of July be rainy weather 'twill rain more or less for four weeks together.*

> *St Swithin's Day, if thou dost rain, for forty days it will remain;*
> *St Swithin's Day, if thou be fair, for forty days 'twell rain nae mair*

> *A wet summer always precedes a cold and stormy winter.*

Nevertheless, fine weather at the end of July prepares the cornfields for harvesting, and in a few hot, dusty hours the harvest can be gathered in … a task that a century before, would have occupied the people of a whole village for days.

## The Turning of the Year

There is a distinct turning of the year as the countryside begins its change from green to gold, and our thoughts turn to the preparation for winter in order to keep the family well fed during the cold months.

**Then:** Baking Lammas bread.
**Now:** Haymaking in the meadows.

**The Circle ritual for July should incorporate bread, salt, wine and (olive) oil as part of the offerings.** A suitable ritual could ask for the blessings of health and prosperity for the immediate family … it is also a time to think about renewing the protection around your home.

## Birch Magic

At night, when its silvery bark glimmers in the moonlight, the birch creates a majestic yet ethereal image. The tree's loose, paper-like bark was held sacred by early man and excavations of Neolithic and Mesolithic grave-mounds reveal that rolls of birch bark were interred alongside the corpse, although their exact significance remains a mystery.

The birch is the first tree of the Ogham alphabet and, although it was listed as a 'tree of high estate', it was referred to by the Celts as one of the 'peasant trees'. Birch twigs were often used for the brush part of a witch's besom, although it was more usual to use the timber as the handle of the broom. Birch twigs were traditionally used to 'beat the boundaries', an annual ceremony to mark out territory and later, parish boundaries. All over Europe the birch tree is associated with renewal and the return of summer. Its boughs were used as decoration at pagan festivals and the Maypole, was often made from a birch tree. After the Beltaine festival, the pole would be taken down and kept in the stable or farm yard as a protection for the household and the livestock.

The birch was esteemed in herbal remedies and during the reign of James I, Sir Hugh Platt tells of a treatment to remove freckles from the hands and face:

> the sap that issueth out of the birch tree in great abundance, being opened in March with a receiver of glass set under the boring, doth perform most excellent and maketh the skin very clear. This sap will also dissolve pearls — a secret not known to many, it being close concealed from most.

In the Middle Ages, sap from the silver birch was a major source of sugar throughout eastern Europe and was fermented to make wine, spirits and vinegar. Revered by the Celts as a sacred tree, it was believed to drive out evil spirits, hence the 'birching' of criminals and the insane. During the Middle Ages, a bundle of birch rods symbolises the authority of the local magistrate.

## The Witch's Loaf Spell

*It is believed to be unlucky to turn a loaf upside down, after helping oneself from it. If you turn a loaf of bread the wrong way you will turn someone out of the house, or bring ill luck.* Traditional witches are honour-bound by the 'breaking of bread' and the ill-wishing of anyone breaking that trust can be reversed by placing the offender's name skewered with a rusty pin or nail, inside a new loaf. The loaf can then be fed to carrion birds (making sure they cannot injure themselves on the nail); or burned in a very hot oven making sure it is placed upside down.

Chapter Eleven

# August — Harvest Moon

**August is the Harvest Moon – although some Old Craft traditions use this name for the full moon following the Autumn Equinox — represented by the Hazel. This is a holy tree connected with fire, fertility, knowledge, divination and poetry. It is a favourite wood for a water-diviner's rod and one of the nine sacred woods used in the Beltain Fire. The Irish-Gaelic and Scottish-Gaelic names for the month, *Lunasa* and *Lunasdel*, refer to the festival of *Lughnasadh* (in honour of the pagan god Lugh) on 1st August, which became synonymous with Lammas in traditional witchcraft. The Anglo-Saxons also referred to it as the 'Harvest-month' or *Weodmonath* (month of weeds). In the 14th century misericord calendar, it was shown as the time for reaping and the start of the harvest.**

During the autumn of 1621, the settlers at Plymouth Colony gathered to give thanks for the harvest after their first year in the New World. That was America's first Thanksgiving, but it has its roots in the traditional Harvest Supper — or Harvest Home — of the English farming community. In truth, the practice of holding a Harvest Festival church service was only established in the 19th century in an attempt to control the Harvest Home celebrations, which the Church of the time considered too raucously pagan!

Harvest celebrations were some of the holiest of the pagan year. Traditionally, the harvest continued for most of August from Lammas, when bread was made from the first corn to be cut; right through to the last fruits being gathered in early September. Any witch worth her salt would be bottling fruit, making pickles and jams, drying herbs and preparing potions from the natural harvest in the hedgerows for the months ahead when fresh ingredients would not be available.

A typical 17th century Harvest Supper would have consisted of ... 'puddings, bacon or boiled beef, flesh or apple pies, and then cream brought in platters ... hot cakes and ale ...'. *A Witch's Treasury for Hearth & Garden,* however, brought the menu up to date with home-made soup, honey-glazed ham, apple pie with cream and a selection of cheeses, served with celery, accompanied by good beer, cider or robust red wine.

This is a perfect time to gather friends and family together for a celebratory supper in a spirit of thanksgiving, whether we are urban or rural dwellers, market trader or stock market trader. And although the American celebration is held on the last Thursday in November, an English Harvest Home is usually held between the Harvest Moon and Autumn Equinox. To set the atmosphere for your party, display any freshly prepared produce for decoration, as this will be your own harvest festival. If you've made jams or pickles, give each guest a small jar as a gesture of sharing. Should your talents lean more towards the arty, give each guest a corn dolly to take home. Corn has long been regarded as the embodiment of productivity and fruitfulness; a simple plait of corn straw tied with ribbon can be hung in the kitchen to insure a productive year to come.

'Thanksgiving' isn't about preserving *ye olde* pagan ways with copious amounts of cider swilling, accompanied by endless verses of *John Barleycorn,* it's about bringing together family and close friends for the purpose of celebration. An annual pilgrimage back to our pagan roots, or to wherever our pagan roots have been transplanted. We can gather around the simple kitchen table, or set the dining room glistening with starched linen, crystal and silver. There is no pre-set formula of observance ... just the willingness to enjoy each other's company, count our blessings and reflect on our *good* fortune.

It would also be nice to think that the modern 'wheel of the year' isn't always driven by the need to use the festivals for spell-casting. Before the end of the meal, make sure everyone has a full glass and propose a toast to your own equivalent of the 'bounty of the harvest', and ask your guests to join you in pouring a libation on the ground outside. Even in financially troubled times, we still have something to be grateful for and if we can re-introduce the spirit of thanksgiving at the turning of the year, we will be re-connecting with the simple faith of our forebears.

The beginning of August (2nd) also marks the date on which the English King, William Rufus was killed whilst out hunting in the New Forest in 1100. Some say he was a pagan sacrifice, while others claim he was assassinated by order of his brother and successor Henry I. There are a number of stories associated with his death, including the account by William of Malmesbury who recorded that the king's blood dripped to the earth during the whole journey, in keeping with the pagan belief that the blood of the 'divine victim' must fall on the ground to ensure the continuing fertility of the land.

The beginning of August marks the old Celtic *Lughnasadh*, the start of the harvesting. The early farmers believed that the spirit of the harvest, the Earth Mother, dwelt within the crop. As the corn was cut from the outside, inwards, the spirit was forced to retreat into the centre. The last stalks of wheat, her final refuge, were woven into the form of a woman. Traditionally, corn dollies were originally made from each harvest by the *men folk* and kept until the following spring. Then the *kern moder* (the original corn dolly) was either burned and ploughed back into the soil or 'released' into the newly-sown seed — returning the spirit of fertility to the earth.

The 7th is the Feast of Cromn Dubh, the Black Bowed One, god of the Underworld. Originally a pre-Celtic god of the harvest, he walks the earth accompanied by two black dogs. This suggests the origins of the diverse folklore legends of large black dogs that roam the British countryside. Perhaps it's a good day to give your canine companion a special treat in honour of the harvest, the word coming from the Old English *haerfest* meaning Autumn.

The 11th marks the end of the Dog Days — the hottest time of the year — and the drawing to a close of summer, followed by the Roman festival of *Vinalia Rustica* on the 19th that celebrates the feast of the grape vine. For all traditional witches it is the time for honouring the god of the harvest with produce taken from the land.

Under the summer sun, corn ripens to gold; wheat turns brown and the barley turns to grey; while oats glow golden as the breeze bends the ripening ears. Scarlet poppies, that have been growing in our fields since Neolithic times, add Monet-like splashes of colour. A touch of yellow can also be found in the hedgerows, while the fruits of blackberry, sloe and elder ripen by the field margin. In the orchards much of the fruits are now ready for gathering.

August is sometimes looked upon as a summer month and sometimes an autumn month, depending on whether the seasons are early or late, or in which part of the country we live. Long ago, when Britain was predominantly a rural country and most of the population worked on the land, August was considered to be the first month of autumn. In fact, in medieval England, August was an autumn month because it *was* the start of the harvest — midsummer having fallen on 21st June. Although this is the harvest month, not all of the corn is cut; in some parts of the country where the season falls later, it may not be fully ripe. The Harvest Home will be delayed until the last field has been cut, but already the house martins are collecting in large numbers ready to travel south … and by the end of the month, the swifts will have gone.

## The Hearth Fire
In some rural areas, the tradition of the Harvest Home supper still takes place. A real harvest supper offers all the things that

would have been found waiting at suppertime in a farmhouse kitchen after a long day out in the fields. Traditionally, the supper would have been eaten outside, or around the kitchen table, as this would have been a 'working' meal. Tables would have been piled high with home-cured ham and game pie, with plenty of home-grown vegetables, pickles and crusty bread. The following is a modern harvest-supper recipe from Lincolnshire:

## Lincolnshire Potato Cheesecake

*Short crust pastry to cover an 8 inch flan tin.*
*Filling:*
*8 oz hot, cooked potatoes*
*Salt*
*Pinch of nutmeg (optional)*
*4 oz softened butter*
*4 oz caster sugar*
*2 eggs, beaten*
*Grated rind and juice of a lemon*

Sieve hot potatoes with salt and nutmeg. Add butter, sugar, eggs, grated rind and lemon juice. Beat thoroughly together. Prick the base of the pastry case and fill almost to the top with the mixture. Bake on a middle shelf at Gas 6 (400F/200C) for 15 minutes, or until filling is set. Brown under the grill if necessary.

or

## Harvest Pudding

*1 packet sage and onion stuffing*
*2 oz grated cheese*
*4 oz cooked ham, chopped*
*2 large eggs, separated*
*Black pepper*
*Pinch of mustard powder*

Prepare packet of sage and onion stuffing as indicated on the packet and allow to cool. Stir in cheese, ham, egg-yolks, some freshly ground black pepper and the mustard powder. Mix well. Beat egg whites until stiff and fold them in lightly with a metal spoon. Turn the mixture into a greased ovenproof dish and bake in a moderate oven, Gas 5 (375F/190C) for 35 minutes. Serve with lightly cooked green vegetables, potatoes or a green salad.

When talking of wild food, it's from August to October that blackberries can be found in the hedgerows, invading wide areas by throwing out spiny shoots that bow to the earth forming natural arches at the root and top. These arches have been used for general magical purposes and healing rituals for centuries — people and animals having been made to crawl beneath the arch to cure various illnesses, including hiccoughs, boils, paralysis and hernias, hence the saying 'to look as if you've been pulled through a hedge backwards'. More practically, the leaves can be crushed and placed on scratches, burns and scalds; they can also be made into a soothing poultice for haemorrhoids.

### Blackberry Curd
**(A preserve resembling lemon curd made with blackberries)**
*2 lb blackberries*
*juice of 2 lemons*
*water to cover*
*2½ lb lump sugar*
*¾ lb apples*
*8oz butter*
*6 eggs*

Simmer together the peeled and cored apples, with the blackberries, in enough water to cover, until the fruit is soft. Pour through a sieve into a double boiler; add the juice of two lemons, the butter and the sugar. When it has all dissolved, add the well-beaten eggs and continue cooking until the mixture thickens, stirring all the time. Pour into sterilised, warmed jars and seal as for jam.

In some parts of the country the Faere Folk are said to have spoiled the fruit. 'Never pick berries past the last day of September, the pookies are sure to have pittled on them,' warned one grandmother every year. These superstitions appear to have arisen from the fact that with the onset of heavy dews and fine frosts, mildew begins to affect the late berries, making them unfit for eating. Witches and old country people were probably fully aware of this but it was a good way of making sure that no bad fruit was included in the crop.

Elderberries are rich in Vitamin C and can be used to make jams, jellies and a strong, flavoured, dark ruby wine. The extracted juice of the berries can be taken to relieve colic and rheumatism, as well as to fight off colds and flu.

## Elderberry & Apple Jelly

*Equal weights of elderberries and sliced apples*
*(not peeled or cored)*
*Sugar*

Cook the elderberries and apples separately, with enough water just to cover the fruit. Simmer till tender and broken up. Test for pectin and if the set is poor reduce further. Strain the fruit through a scalded jelly bag. Measure the juices, mix, return to the pan and heat. Add ¾ lb sugar for every pint of juice. Stir till dissolved. Boil rapidly till setting point is reached. Pour into heated jars and allow to cool before sealing.

When harvesting all this wild bounty remember to leave a suitable offering under the shrub or tree from where the fruit has been picked. A handful of brown breadcrumbs or sugar would be appropriate.

## Weatherwise

The hottest days of the year often fall in the month of August but farmers welcome such weather:

- *Dry August and warm doth harvest no harm.*
- *August rain gives honey and wine*

It may, however, warn of a hard winter to come:

- *If the first week of August be warm, the winter will be long and white.*

The wise witch makes the most of the good weather and spends as much time as possible out in the fields. This is a good time for divination as there are a large number of fauna about in the newly cut meadows, and large billowing clouds in the summer sky.

## The Turning of the Year

If a farmer's year can be said to begin at any fixed point, it is at the time when one crop is harvested and preparations for the next one begin. Harvest usually begins at the end of July/beginning of autumn (hence Lammas) generally with winter barley or oats. August is the main harvest month in the south; September is the month in the north (and in the south in a wet summer).

**Then:** Reaping.
**Now:** Wheat and barley are golden ripe.

**There has always been a spiritual quality surrounding harvest time and the Circle ritual for August should be a celebration of**

the good things that have happened during the year. *Lughnasadh* is a sympathetic magical ritual designed to guarantee that there would be enough food during the winter, by displaying and eating the finest of the harvest. It is a time for consideration of matters concerning money and to think of the older members of the family.

## Hazel Magic

The hazel has been associated with wisdom, magic and divination for centuries and the carrying of a hazel wand conferred not only wisdom but the power of eloquence on the bearer. The most potent hazel wand should be cut on Midsummers' morning. Although we think of the forked hazel twig as the diviners' rod these days, a straight hazel wand can also be used for water divining and to attract rain — also to find veins of metal. To protect a seedbed from the attention of birds, insects and the Faere Folk draw on it with a hazel wand a cross, followed by a heart then another cross.

An incense of the fruit or twigs can be used for any positive purpose, particularly to strengthen mental powers including magical will and concentration also to give the stamina needed to complete long or complicated rituals. Hazel is associated with Elemental Fire, and was one of the nine sacred woods used to kindle the magical Need Fire at Beltane.

Weave a wreath of hazel leaves and twigs and wear it during any spells to gain your most secret wishes and desires. The hazel nut can be used in love philters, when they will awaken the recipient to the virtues of the sender. Hazel leaves can be used to banish an unwanted lover, charm a leaf by simply chanting the name of the person then *Depart! Depart! Depart!'* The leaf can then either be burnt, or posted to your lover (there is no need to put in any letter in the envelope), or slipped in their pocket. Hazel nuts make a wonderful gift for a new bride — as long as she wants plenty of children!

## A Witch's Tincture of Magical Protection

*Woodland Mother, black as night, Silver Goddess, shining bright*
*Queen of Arrows, elfin sprite, Banish evil, give us calm*
*Keep all safe and free from harm. Brew, now, this protective charm!*

Pick nine blackberries by the light of the Full Moon. When you get home the rest of the procedure must be performed by candlelight, or by the light of the Moon herself, as you sit by a window open to the night breeze — do not use any artificial light. Express the juice and place it in a small bottle made of coloured glass. Half fill the bottle with pure spring water then top up with brandy. Put the lid on and shake the mixture as you chant the above three times. The whole plant is protective, so if it is not the right time of year for collecting the berries, and you have the need, collect nine leaves instead.

# Chapter Twelve

# September — Hunter's Moon

September brings the Hunter's Moon — when meat stocks were set aside for the winter and cattle culled to conserve food and fodder — and represented by the Apple. This is one of the sacred trees that possesses magical powers and when its fruit is cut across, displays the magical sign of the pentagram. The old name for Glastonbury Avalon means 'the place of apple trees' and it is customary for a Samhain Apple to be eaten for good luck — hence the traditional party game of 'bobbing for apples'. Some of the Celtic names of the month are also linked to the harvest — the Welsh *Medi* means 'reaping' and the Scottish-Gaelic *Sultuine* means 'plenty'. The Anglo-Saxons called it *Gerstmonath* or Barley-month with reference to the harvest of that crop, the main ingredient of the favourite alcoholic beverage. In the 14th century misericord calendar, it was shown as the time for cutting the corn for malting. The Autumn Equinox falls on or around the 21st and the constellation of Orion (the Hunter) reappears in the dark before dawn by the end of the month.

This really is the time of Keats' 'season of mists and mellow fruitfulness'. In the orchards and hedgerows, branches are laden with fruit although in country-lore heavy crops of berries on the elder, rowan, holly and blackberry are said to be the signs of a bad winter to come. If the birds strip the berries early in the season, it means the winter will be mild but if the berries are left relatively untouched until the colder weather then prepare for a long, cold winter.

In rare cases, you may find wild filberts or cobnuts, one of the few indigenous nuts of Britain, which the Romans used to flavour roast duck. During medieval times, they were used in cakes, bread, confectionery and liqueurs, while oil from the nuts was used in cooking. At the beginning of the season, the husks and shells are still green and were often picked at this stage; as the season progresses into October, the nuts ripen and turn brown. Cobnuts resemble large hazelnuts but have a much sweeter taste similar to sweet chestnuts.

**But not all of Nature's harvest is bountiful.** Throughout the year, there is a profusion of berries and wild fungi that have provided additional food in times of shortage but many of the most appealing plants are poisonous. And witches have always been knowledgeable about poison

## Poisonous and Inedible Berries

Hawthorn: inedible (when raw)
Guelder rose: poisonous
White bryony: poisonous
Black bryony: poisonous
Rowan: inedible (when raw)
Spindle tree: poisonous
Holly: poisonous
Deadly nightshade: poisonous
Rose hips: inedible (when raw)
Woody nightshade: poisonous
Black nightshade: poisonous
Privet: poisonous
Blackthorn sloe: inedible (when raw)

The spindle gets its name from the fact that from prehistoric times, the thin stems from this tree were been used for spinning thread. There are small, insignificant greenish flowers in May but the crowning glory of the spindle tree is the profusion of bright pink, four-lobed berries that make it one of the most beautiful of autumn fruits, despite its poisonous nature.

Equally as deadly, by the end of September the hedgerows and woods will be displaying an impressive collection of wild fungi right through into October. There are some 3,000 species, of which about 50 are edible but even if you don't fancy eating them, these strange variants provide interesting colour and texture to the autumn tapestry. There's lots of folklore pertaining to the identification of wild mushrooms from being able to peel edible ones or poisonous ones turning blue when touched with a penny (a pre-decimal penny, that is) but the best advice of all is to leave well alone if you don't know what you're looking for. Invest in a reliable guide and be safe rather than sorry: but even illustrations may often be misleading

The three most lethal are the Death Cap (*amanita phalloides*) found in deciduous woodland, mainly under oak and beech; developing a distinct sweet, honey smell when fresh or an unpleasant ammonia smell when old. Destroying Angel (*amanita virosa*) found in coniferous forests also has a sweet, honey smell. Panther Cap (*amanita pantherina*) found in both coniferous and deciduous woodland but has no distinctive smell. All these are highly toxic and can kill. Or as one countryman said: 'Eat half a Death Cap and it's not a case of whether you may die, but how long it will take you to die.'

Other poisonous mushrooms are the False Fairy Ring (*clitocybe dealbata*) found on grassy slopes and in domestic gardens, with a distinctly mealy smell; Yellow Stainer (*agaricus xanthodermus*) found on forest fringes, in parks and meadows, which smells unpleasantly of carbolic when bruised; and the Common Ink Cap (*coprinus atramentarius*). In true country-lore tradition, the common ink cap *is* edible — but it contains a chemical that reacts strongly with alcohol that can prove fatal.

There are, however, numerous varieties that *are* edible and which have medicinal properties. The common field mushroom was thought by Culpeper to be: 'Roasted and applied in a poultice, or boiled with white lily roots, and linseed, in milk, they ripen boils and abscesses better than any preparation that can be made'. While Gerard wrote that it was 'much used against the inflammation and all other soreness of the throat, being boiled in milk, steeped in beer, vinegar, or any other convenient liqueur'.

From Roman times, edible mushrooms have been cooked as vegetables, or included in soups, sauces, pickles and meat dishes. Some varieties were threaded on strings and hung up to dry for use over winter. The following is a filling for sandwiches, which is quick and easy to make and will keep in the refrigerator for two to three days. For a tasty snack, spread the filling on slices of lightly toasted brown bread and put under the grill to melt the filling.

## Mushroom Sandwich Filling

*1 lb cream cheese*
*1 teaspoon salt*
*½ teaspoon black pepper*
*2 hard-boiled eggs, finely chopped*
*2 pickled cucumbers, very finely chopped*
*2 tablespoons chopped fresh chive (or jack by the hedge)*
*2 oz mushrooms, wiped clean and finely chopped*

In a large mixing bowl, mash all the ingredients together with a wooden spoon until they are well combined. Cover the bowl with aluminium foil and place in the refrigerator. Use as required.

In Britain, cereals including wheat, oats, barley and rye are collectively known as corn (In America, corn applies only to maize, originally known as Indian corn) and as we have seen, it was considered propitious to pay homage to the last sheaf of corn cut at the end of the harvest. The custom is a survival of pagan rites originating in the Middle East 7000 years ago, which were observed in order to appease the corn spirit, or fertility goddess who took her final refuge in that last sheaf. The sheaf was garlanded and carried home in procession, and kept through the winter months in the farmhouse or church to ensure a good harvest next year.

Corn dollies are made from this sheaf and kept in the house, or given away to friends to perpetuate the success of the harvest in the coming year. The dollies are made in various traditional patterns, which vary from village to village. For example, the Suffolk horseshoe, the Staffordshire knot and the horn of plenty of Northamptonshire are among the typical good luck symbols.

As we have already seem, some witches still like to call the Autumn Equinox the beginning of autumn and although there is no official first calendar day of any of the seasons, both the traditional witch and the countryman feel the pull of the changing tides. This is the time of the dying year and when we walk the fields and woodlands on a regular basis, we cannot avoid being confronted by death and decay at every turn. Nevertheless, it is a spiritually up-lifting time and we know that with the turning of the year, spring *will* follow winter no matter how cold the months to come.

## The Hearth Fire

Although the long hot summers are a disaster for pasture and grazing, it often produces an abundance of wild fruits, with hedgerows heavy with crab apples, sloes elderberries, rosehips, blackberries and elderberries. Most of these are too bitter to be edible on their own and are much improved for being made into vinegars, chutneys, jams and liqueurs to use as accompaniments to food during the winter months.

The weather is cooler in the evenings and mornings and within its shadow, there is a chillness that haunts the autumn woods. There is an indescribable 'scent' that heralds autumn, which any witch will recognise. This is the time for a light lunch or home-from-school snack by the fire, and this farmhouse recipe is ideal:

### Tomato Rarebit

*1 cup strained tomatoes*
*½ cup soft breadcrumbs*
*Salt and pepper*
*½ lb grated cheese*
*Toast*

A variation can have a poached egg served on top. Or a mixture of 8 oz cheese with 2 slices of Welsh bacon and a small onion all minced and mixed together. This was spread on toast and baked in a hot oven until bubbling. Place all the ingredients in a saucepan. Cook until smooth, stirring constantly. Serve at once on hot toast.

Crab Apple Jelly is an ideal accompaniment to roast pork, or alternatively the fruit can be used to make homemade wine. Old country recipes often say that the addition of a couple of crab apples make all the difference to an apple tart.

### Crab Apple Jelly
**(This is an ideal substitute for apple-sauce and can be served with roast pork and cold meat.)**

*4lb crab apples*
*lemon peel or root ginger*
*Sugar*

Wash the apples and cut up without peeling or coring — just remove any bad portions. Barely cover with water (about 2-3 pints) and simmer with the chosen flavouring until tender and well mashed (about 1 hour). Strain through a scalded jelly bag. Bring the strained juice to the boil and test for pectin. Add the sugar (usually 1 lb sugar to every pint of juice). Stir to dissolve. Boil briskly till setting point is reached. Pour into heated jars and allow to cool before sealing.

In our hedges, there are two varieties of crab apples. *Malus sylvestris* is the native species and has small yellow fruit, while *malus mitis*, known in certain areas as a 'wilding', looks more like a normal apple, having descended from ancient cultivated stock. Both are too bitter to eat raw but simmered with sugar to make a jelly or 'cheese', they are an excellent accompaniment to cold meats and cheeses.

## Crab Apple Cheese

    5 lb crab apples
    1½ pints good cider
    Sugar
    3 cloves
    pinch of nutmeg
    pinch of cinnamon

Roughly chop the apples and simmer with cider until soft. Squeeze through a sieve and weigh. Add an equal amount of sugar, then the spices, and simmer until thick.

    Pour into sterilised jars and seal. Serve with port or cheese.

The Autumnal Equinox is also a perfect time to combine the elements of the Hunter's Moon and the sacred symbolism in the form of an apple and pork casserole. This can be served in the dish in which it is cooked and provides a good family lunch, or informal supper-party dish that can be made with inexpensive cuts of pork.

## Pork & Apple Casserole

    *2 lb lean, pork, boned*
    *1 tablespoon butter, softened*
    *2 medium sized onions, chopped*

*½ teaspoon dried sage*
*½ teaspoon salt*
*2 grindings of black pepper*
*2 medium sized cooking apples, peeled, cored and thinly sliced*
*3 tablespoons of water*
*1 ½ potatoes, peeled*
*2 tablespoons hot milk*
*1 tablespoon butter, cut into pieces.*

Remove any excess fat from the pork and then cut into cubes. Grease a large ovenproof casserole with the butter. Put the onions, sage, salt and pepper into a mixing bowl and stir to mix. Into the casserole, place about one-third of the pork cubes and cover them with one-half of the onion mixture and with half of the sliced apples. Continue to fill the casserole with the remaining pork, onions and apples finishing with a layer of pork. Add the water. Cover the casserole and cook in the oven (Gas 3, 170C, 325F) for 2-2 ½ hours or until the pork is tender. About 30 minutes before the pork is cooked, boil the potatoes and mash with the hot milk and butter. Spread over the pork and dot with pieces

Rowan Jelly is also a perfect accompaniment with cold venison or game:

### Rowan Jelly
*3 lb cooking apples*
*5 lb rowan berries*
*3 pints water*
*4 lb sugar*

Core and slice the apples. Boil with the berries and water until the mixture forms a thick pulp. Strain through a jelly bag and stir in the sugar. Simmer for 10 minutes, skimming frequently. Pour into sterilised jars and seal.

A traditional drink for the coming Autumn Equinox (or next month's Samhain celebrations) is what is known in country circles as 'Lambswool' — which takes its name from the fluffy apple puree that bursts from the fruit and floats on top.

## Lambswool

Pour a bottle of good cider into a large saucepan, spice it with a good grating of nutmeg, a couple of pinches of powdered ginger and add sugar to taste. Put it on a low heat. Meanwhile, put a dozen or so crab apples in a roasting tin with a scattering of sugar and a tablespoon or two of water. Bake at 200F/400C/Gas mark 6 for about 20 mins. They are ready when they burst and should be tossed into the now steaming hot cider with the fluffy white interiors popped out almost like popcorn. Drink the cider and pulp, leaving the apples in the glass.

The natural harvest can be extremely bountiful but don't strip the trees and bushes ... leave some fruit for the wild birds and animals that will need it to survive the winter.

## Weatherwise

Everyone hopes for temperate weather in September, so that crops will not be damaged before they can be gathered in: *September blow soft, till fruit be in the loft,* while the three days preceding the Autumnal Equinox are supposed to determine the weather for the following three months.

Swallows gather in flocks over farmland in readiness for the long flight to Africa for the winter. Their leaving was thought to coincide with the Autumn Equinox; or Michaelmas on the 29th September, the date traditionally marking the end of harvesting. If the swallows leave early then it is taken to mean that bad weather is on the way.

## The Turning of the Year

The Autumnal Equinox is the halfway mark between summer and winter. September 22nd is the most common date, but it can also fall on the 21st or 23rd depending on where we are in the leap-year cycle. The name derives from the Latin *aequi* meaning 'equal' and *nox* meaning 'night' — on this date (and at the Vernal Equinox), day and night are theoretically the same length throughout the world, with the sun above the horizon for 12 hours.

**Then:** Corn for malting.
**Now**: The harvest is just in.

**The Circle ritual for the month of September should observe the fundamental time of balance between light and dark.** It is a time to complete old business in preparation for the winding down of the year. Take the opportunity to practice divination by leaves — or botanomancy. Words pertinent to your situation are written on leaves that are then exposed to the wind. The leaves left behind contain the response.

## Apple Magic

The folklore associated with apples appears mostly to do with determining romantic outcomes and finding a marriage partner. The apple has always been regarded as a holy tree and since earliest times it has been considered very unlucky to destroy apple trees or an orchard. On the opposite side of the coin, it was said to bring luck to the household if several apples were left on the ground after the harvest to keep the Faere Folk happy. While apple orchards have long been regarded as places where the realms of the Faere Folk meet the mundane world. Mistletoe being the 'golden bough' and although more traditionally associated with oak trees, it is more commonly found on apple trees. The apple was one of the seven Chieftain trees and under

Brehon law, the unlawful cutting down of an apple tree had to be paid for with a life.

Burnt indoors, apple wood will perfume the whole house, which certainly makes it one of the woods suitable for the Beltaine fire. Some traditional witches will also use apple juice or cider as a libation in their magical workings and seasonal festivities. Falling apple blossoms can be used for divination in spring. Catch a falling petal and you can use it to make a wish, or catch a dozen and ensure a happy year to come. Make it thirteen if you're counting by lunar months.

Apples also make an appearance at Harvest Home suppers and Samhain when 'bobbing' is a popular entertainment. To use the time to call back spirits of those who have passed from this world during the previous year, choose an unblemished apple and as the clock finishes striking midnight, stick twelve new pins into the apple. Place the apple in the fire and call the name of the person you wish to contact.

There are numerous spells and charms that involve various parts of the tree (including divination with the blossom), all of which have survived as 'love' spells. With a little bit of imagination, most of these can be rendered into useful spells and cast in whatever manner you wish! The popular rhyme 'an apple a day keeps the doctor away', is a throw-back to the ancient belief that the fruit was a cure-all. In more recent times, apples have been found to contain health-giving properties that help fight cancer and heart disease.

In Celtic mythology, the apple was known as the Silver Bough (the mistletoe that traditionally grows on it is the Golden Bough), sacred to the moon and all lunar energies. It is the special fruit of Otherworld and the pagan festival of Samhain was sometimes called the Feast of Apples. Samhain (or All Hallows) is a good time to observe some those of traditional spells.

Chapter Thirteen

# The Witch's Wildlife

The dictionary definition of a 'totem' refers to any species of a living or inanimate thing regarded by those within a local group or tribe with superstitious respect as 'an outward symbol of an existing intimate unseen relation'. And it is here in the open fields we find the birds that have a long association with traditional witchcraft — the *Corvidae* family that includes rooks, ravens, choughs, crows, jackdaws, jays and magpies.

The crow, rook and jackdaw are all outwardly similar members of the crow family, so similar in fact, that even many country people refer to them all simply as 'crows'. The old country saying that *'one rook is a crow; a flock of crows are rooks'* is generally true except for occasions when juvenile rooks feed alone and crows (especially youngsters) do form small flocks. They are all common species on agricultural land (except for the jay, chough and raven), although in northern Britain and Ireland there is a handsome sub-species called the hooded crow.

**Crow:** Plumage uniformly dull black and may be distinguished from the rook by the absence of white skin at the base of the bill. Usually a solitary bird, it is seen flying alone or in pairs, except where feeding or roosting places attract them in numbers. In general crows are not liked in British superstition and the belief in their basic unluckiness was mention by many leading literary figures including Chaucer and Shakespeare. **Hooded crow:** Grey plumage on back and under-parts. Resident in the north and Ireland, and a winter visitor in autumn and winter in southern Britain.

**Chough:** A rare seabird, similar to a jackdaw but with scarlet legs and a curved scarlet bill, that inhabits the cliffs on the western seaboard. It features in West Country and Channel Islands folklore, where it was linked with witchcraft because witches were believed to wear red stockings!

**Jackdaw:** Black with a grey patch on nape and cheeks, with startling blue eyes. They also get a bad press in British superstition: at best, they were unlucky, and often as a sign of impending death or disaster.

**Jay:** A very handsome bird with pinkish-brown plumage, black and white on the head, and a bright blue patch on the wings. Unlike the rest of the family, it is a shy bird and often only glimpsed as a flash of blue in woods and copses. The bird was first recorded as being an evil omen in the 1600s.

**Magpie:** Unmistakable with its glossy black and white plumage and long graduated tail. There is a general dislike of magpies in Britain and Irish folklore, although one of the oldest superstitions is that the chatter indicates the coming of a stranger, with the earliest known reference dating from 1159AD. The bird was, however, revered by the Iceni.

**Raven:** The largest member of the crow family and the rarest. Its bad reputation has been held since classical times and both Virgil and Pliny commented on its ominous nature. The bird was, however, sacred to the gods Odin and Bran.

**Rook:** Glossy black plumage and gregarious by nature, rooks roost, feed and fly in large numbers. The traditional view of the rook is less ominous than that of the crow, and in some places, they are considered lucky to have around.

As usual, with folklore *vs* witchcraft, anything that had been traditionally associated with charms or spells to avert ill luck, has subsequently been labelled an antidote *against* witches and the Faere Folk. Here we need to look *behind* the superstitions and learn to extract the kernel of truth behind the protective niceties of folklore.

The personal totem is one that has been part of every culture from the Stone Age right through history, and up to its modern use in heraldry. This sacred fauna can be acquired, or even chosen by the magical practitioner (some witches use the name of an animal or bird as part of their own magical persona). Sometimes the totem animal is recognised when a creature appears to have formed some sort of mystical link with the witch. For example, we might find that if we have a difficult decision to make and notice that there is the unexpected daytime appearance of a bat, or owl, or fox — or a particular animal behaving out of its normal routine. Alternatively, the image can make itself known by appearing with unusual or distinctive colouring. Often white or albino animals are magical signs and these might appear in meditation, dreams, or even caught for an instant in the glare of the headlights as we drive through the night.

Normally, we would acquire an image that seems appropriate either to our magical aspirations, or one with which we feel an affinity. The vast majority of us, of course, will live in a part of the world where the likelihood of encountering *any* of this indigenous wildlife on a daily basis is pretty remote. We may, however, encounter these images on television, in a magazine or newspaper, in 'junk mail' that arrives unexpectedly, or a statue/picture/book found at a car boot sale.Sacred images do not necessarily have to be *living* creatures, they can also be represented by symbols.

A witch's personal universe does not allow for coincidences and should the totem image appear — in whatever form — it should be noted and recorded, even if the significance isn't apparent at that precise moment in time. Messages and warnings filter through to us from other planes in all manner of guises and it is up to us to receive and interpret them to the best of our ability. If we chose to ignore them, waiting for something more profound to appear, our 'guardians' may not bother next time! So if, for example, we identify with any member of the *Corvidae* family, then that bird will become our 'totem' and an integral part of our daily lives — even if we live in an urban area.

*Corvidae* feathers are easily come by and can help establish a magical link with the bird. For the less squeamish, animal concretions are stones supposedly found in some part of the body of an animal or bird, and which contain the magical essence of the creature in concentrated form. Such stones were worn as amulets, or pulverised for use in potions and other recipes. Traditionally, they are obtained by leaving the carcass to be eaten by ants, or by suspending it so that the stone dropped out of its mouth. Similarly, the skull or bones of a dead animal or bird can be left on an anthill to be cleaned and subsequently used for magical or shamanic purposes.

## Lucid Dreaming Exercise

This is a half-waking, half-dream state where the witch is fully conscious and aware of his/her surroundings but still able to receive images or impressions from the astral. The astral image is often superimposed over the immediate surroundings like a double-exposure on a photograph, and is best performed whilst sitting in a patch of bright sunlight either outdoors, or at home relaxing in an armchair. Like meditation and pathworking, this technique can be used to solve problems and/or receive guidance/instruction.

The sunlight helps us to relax and here we *do* focus on the problem or difficulties that are causing us concern. After a while, the view within our immediate vicinity will become blurred or distorted, and in this half-dream, we begin to see images with a veil-like quality. The images may provide an answer, or we may even encounter our totem animal immediately after we 'earth' ourselves. Again, with constant use, we become more receptive to the thoughts and impulses that can often solve those problematic situations that cause us stress and worry.

## The Witch's Wish

*On All-Hallows Eve nuts should be thrown into the fire, and wishes expressed in secret. If the nut blazes the wish will be granted, but if not it 'dies away'.* A witch asks that the spirits will grant the request, and in return, they are offered a small libation. This is a free will offering that accepts the spirits too, have their Will, and may grant the witch's request ... or not. A witch has the right to ask, but not necessarily to receive.

# Chapter Fourteen

# October — Falling Leaf Moon

**October is the Falling Leaf Moon that heralds the dying of the year at *Samhain* — represented by the Blackthorn. Considered by many to be an ominous tree because a blackthorn staff is sometimes used as the altar stang when a cursing or banishment is taking place. The tree sports some barbarous spikes and gives its name to the 'blackthorn winter' — a sudden, bitterly cold spell in the spring when the tree is in flower. The Anglo-Saxons called it *wynmonath* — the time of treading the wine-vats. Or *Winterfyllith*, referring to a calendar in which the full moon of this month marked the beginning of winter, although officially, the Hunter's Moon is the second full moon after the Autumn Equinox. The Irish-Gaelic name also makes reference to the changing of the seasons: *Deireadh Fomhair* meaning 'the end of autumn'. In the 14th century misericord calendar, it was shown as the time for gathering acorns to feed the pigs.**

This month shows the British countryside at its most glorious as the sun sinks lower in the sky. The clocks go back, the mornings are misty and the nip in the darkening evenings warns of the cold and damp to come. By now the trees are ablaze with gold and bronze as the leaves get ready to fall, and ribbons of mist wrap themselves around the bole of the oak and beech. In hedgerows overrun by old man's beard, berries of every hue glisten in the weakening sun's rays, waiting for the first frosts to scour the fruit. Nevertheless, there is often a brief interlude of warm weather.

**All Hallown Summer**: A second summer that sets in around All-Hallows (or St Luke's summer — St Luke's Day is 18th October), which is now more popularly referred to as an Indian Summer. Shakespeare uses the term in *Henry IV*.i.2 'Farewell, thou latter spring; farewell, All-Hallown Summer!'

**Second** or **Autumnal Summer**: Said to last 30 days and begins about the time that the sun enters **Scorpio** (23rd October). It is variously called St Martin's summer; All Saints' or St Luke's little summer. Shakespeare refers to them as: 'Expect St Martin's summer; halcyon days,' in *Henry VI*, 1.2.

**Indian Summer:** A short spell of extremely fine weather and often occurs during October and the first part of November. The description was introduced during the 19th century from North America as this was the time when the Native Americans stored crops in preparation for the winter.

Commonly found on roadsides, pasture, wood edges and stream banks, the teasel stands proud over the dying foliage of other plants. In medieval times, the water that collected in the stems was reputed to possess soothing, healing properties. The hooked spines on the ends of the bracts were used for fluffing up cloth and it was often referred to as 'brushes and combs' — today it is more likely to be found as part of an indoor flower arrangement, or grown in the garden to encourage goldfinches that love to eat the autumn seeds.

The Anglo Saxon name for ribwort plantain is *weg-braede*, which means 'way-breath', so called because it grows by waysides and tracks, the flowering heads nodding in the autumn wind. It was also one of the nine sacred herbs of the Anglo-Saxons, who used its leaves in poultices to heal wounds, blisters and bites. Widely distributed over grasslands and by fresh water, the leaves should be gathered during the flowering period.

## Tincture Preparation

*1 part herb to five parts liquid of which 25%*
*should be alcohol based.*

Put 8 oz of cut dried herb, or 1 lb of the fresh leaves into a large jar. Pour 1¼ pints of vodka and ½ pint water over the herb and close the jar tightly. Keep the container in a warm place for two weeks, shaking well once a day. Strain of the liquid through a muslin cloth suspended over a bowl. Pour the tincture into a dark glass bottle and keep in a cool place away from direct sunlight. Stored correctly, tinctures will keep for up to three years. Use on wounds, bites and stings.

In the woods, mixed flocks of the tit family (blue, great, coal and long-tailed), goldcrests and tree-creepers are working together through the oak trees in search of insects. In the fields and hedgerows, other kinds of birds flock together in order to feed well in the shortening hours of daylight. This behaviour is not just about feeding — it's also about protection, with hundreds of pairs of eyes looking out for predators. Many of the smaller birds, like the greenfinch or chaffinch, have bright bars on their wings and if just one bird spots a predator, the flash of the wing bars as it flies up alerts the rest of the flock to danger.

This early-warning defence system also helps the birds to feed well because a single bird must always be alert to danger. Observation shows that the birds in the middle spend less time looking around because they can depend on the 'out-riders' to warn them of danger. This pattern often changes by a leap-frogging system, whereby each one gets the opportunity to feeds and guard.

Elegant magpies, long believed to be birds of ill omen in later cultures, were welcomed by the Iceni as they warned that wolves were roaming the countryside. The bird's services were honoured each year by the placing of a tribute of heather near the nest. The bird was originally referred to as a *pie*, but during the Elizabethan era the pre-fix of *mag* was added — a term that previously identified the female bird.

This is a cunning and intelligent bird and its fighting abilities are superb. Countryman Philip Clucas wrote:

With a swift aerial attack, using only their sharp beak to strike, they are one of the few creatures capable of killing adders for food. This display of courage was greatly admired during the days of cock-fighting, and hen's eggs were sometimes placed in a magpie's nest in the hope that the chick would inherit some of the foster parent's bravery, and thus be victorious in the cock-ring.

Superstitious people still react to avert bad luck on sight of a single magpie by spitting over their right shoulder or by raising their hat in greeting. The sighting of two birds together, however, is a sign of happiness as the old rhyme goes:

*One for sorrow, two for joy,*
*Three for a wedding, four for a boy.*

The numbers in the rhyme increase according to different locations although no one knows why grouping of up to 30 birds can be seen gathered together in the corner of a field for a 'conference. Many witches have a 'maggie' as their totem animal.

Neither must we overlook the ghostly-white flash seen in the half-light or dawn or dusk that announces the presence of the barn owl. The bird is also called the screech owl, due to its loud, shrillshriek, often to be heard as night approaches. Each night the owl patrols its territory, the tip of its wings covered in down, which renders the flight almost silent as it hunts for its prey. The silence of its long, raid wing-beats earned the barn owl its association with supernatural powers, while the feathers were once thought to be one of the ingredients of witches' spells. **For the witch the cry of an owl at the culmination of a magical working is a sign of its success.**

The owl's prey includes rates, that are without doubt, the most disliked of all British wild mammals — and certainly the most destructive. The word rat is derived from the Saxon *raet*, meaning 'the gnawer'. The black rat or Old English rat, is supposed to have arrived in the baggage trains of the returning crusaders and has infested England since medieval times; but has since been largely reduced by the more aggressive brown rat that arrived in this country during the 18th century. In spring the rural population move into the hedgerows and waste ground, but during the damp days of late October, it returns to the shelter of barns and outbuildings.

Should its habitat become unfavourable, the rats will go on a mass migration that can number several thousand, killing anything which gets in their way. Such 'marches' are frequently mentioned in folk-lore and Saxon myths recall that the rat acted as an agent of the gods, bringing retribution to revenge the souls of murder victims. There are many old charms and potions for ridding a property of unwanted rats. For example the following was recited in the north of England and Scotland:

*Rats and mice,*
*Leave this poor person's house,*
*Go on away over to the mill*
*And there you'll all get your fill.*

Another witch charm is to thrust pieces of paper bearing a banishing spell similar to the one above into the rat holes. It has been known for the whole rat population to leave and not return.

## The Hearth Fire
With the cold weather comes the need for traditional cooking

that generates that warm, comforting sensation ... and what better for the time of the Hunter's Moon than a rich game soup.

## Game Soup

*2 pints game stock from carcasses of 2 game birds*
*1 onion*
*1 carrot*
*1 stick celery*
*2 oz butter*
*1 bay leaf*
*Salt and pepper*
*1 oz butter*
*1 oz plain flour*
*1 teaspoons red currant jelly*
*2 teaspoons lemon juice*
*2 tablespoons sherry or red wine*

Peel and chop onion, scrub and chop carrot, wash and slice celery. Melt butter in a large pan and lightly fry the vegetables, turning them in the hot fat until lightly browned. Add stock, bay leaf, salt and pepper, and simmer for 1 hour. Finely chop any meat picked from the carcasses. Melt butter, stir in flour and fry till light brown. Strain the soup and gradually stir in the butter mixture. Bring to the boil and cook for 2-3 minutes. Add the meat and reheat. Add the redcurrant jelly, lemon juice and sherry or red wine. Reheat and serve at once.

The flowers of the blackthorn have been succeeded by hard green fruits, which ripen during the summer to become blue-black sloes, each one coated with a natural dusky bloom. If these are left on the bush until late autumn after the first frost, they do become sweeter and can be used to produce a delightful liqueur. Sloes were also made into jellies, syrups and jams. The following recipes are easy to make:

## Sloe & Apple Jelly

*4lb apples*
*2lb sloes*
*Sugar*

Wash and cut up the apples but do not peel or core. Place in a pan with the sloes, just cover with water and simmer to a pulp. Strain through a scalded jelly bag. Allow 1lb sugar to each pint of juice. Boil till setting point is reached. Pour into heated jars and allow to cool before sealing.

## Traditional Sloe Gin

Half fill clean, dry wine bottles with the fruit previously pricked with a darning needle. An old-fashioned recipe says to add to each 1oz crushed barley sugar, 2-3 drops of almond essence. Fill the bottles with dry, unsweetened gin, cork them securely, and allow them to remain in a moderately warm place for 3 months. At the end of this time, strain the liqueur through fine muslin until quit clear, then bottle. Cork securely and store away in a cool, dry place until required for use. There are regional differences in the preparation of sloe gin, with modern recipes replacing the barley sugar and almond essence with 4ozs of granulated sugar.

## Weatherwise

St Simon and St Jude's Day (28th October) traditionally marks the end of fine weather and the commencement of gales and storms, hence the saying: *A good October and a good blast to blow the hog acorns and mast.* The strong winds bring torrential rain and clouds that rage across the dull, grey sky that herald the time of the Wild Hunt.

## The Turning of the Year

All Hallows, or the Celtic festival of *Samhain* celebrated in

Ireland and Scotland, falls on the 31st October and marks the end of the natural year. From now until the Winter Solstice, Nature is in a moribund state until we celebrate the re-birth of the Sun. Traditionally, this was when the Lord of Misrule was chosen to act as the surrogate king until his sacrificial death at the re-birth of the New Year.

**Then:** Acorns for pigs
**Now:** The field is ploughed for a new crop

**The Circle rite for October traditionally marks the feast of the ancestors, which, if celebrated by the Julian calendar falls on 11th November, to coincide with what we now recognise as Remembrance Day.** Food offerings should be left on altars and doorsteps for the wandering spirits, with candles placed in the windows to help spirits and ancestors to come home.

### Blackthorn Magic

The blackthorn is one of the most powerful trees in Old Craft and because it was an important tree to our pagan ancestors, it is now thought of as having a sinister reputation. Like the whitethorn (hawthorn), the blackthorn has its fair share of associations with the Faere Folk, even having its own appointed Faere guardians. Carrying a leaf, flower or berry in a charm bag will attract the powers of good fortune. Alternatively, fasten a scrap of ribbon or fabric to one of the thorns as you make your wish. The spikes from the blackthorn have long been used to pierce wax images, both for cursing and healing purposes.

The blackthorn sends up erect shoots or suckers from its roots and if these are not cut back they gradually spread to form a dense thicket, which is extremely difficult to remove. In a short time, a large stand of blackthorn can result from just one parent plant. This method of re-colonising, and its Faere Folk connections make an ideal symbol for Elemental Earth. Blackthorn wood is hard and the grain forms intricate patterns of colour. Ireland's fearsome cudgel, the shillelagh, is cut from the main stem of the blackthorn, while the straight stems from younger bushes make handsome walking sticks or staffs.

From medieval times, the tree's medicinal purposes have been recorded: blackthorn flowers were used as a tonic and mild laxative; the leaves as a mouthwash and to stimulate the appetite; the bark to reduce fever; the fruit for bladder, kidney and digestive disorders. According to medieval herbalists, the shrub was held to be 'the regulator of the stomach' since its flowers loosened the bowels and its fruit bound them. The bitter fruit of the blackthorn was made into jellies, syrups, jams, wine and *verjuice* (an acid liquor).

The wood and dried berries can be used as incense in rituals of banishing negativity and so it is as well to collect a small supply of these to dry out and use in a special blend of your own, as and when necessary. Anoint a few twigs of blackthorn with oil and burn a little as incense each day at noon and midnight for seven consecutive days to banish even the most persistent negative forces. Traditionally, blackthorn twigs were woven into a crown of thorns and burned in the cornfields on old New Year's Day, similar to the women's custom of the hawthorn ball. This ceremony was later used as a Christian compromise between the old faith and the new, to ensure that the pagan spirit — the Earth Mother — looked kindly upon the community by bestowing continued fertility upon the land.

Sloes from the blackthorn can be used in wart-charming. Rub the wart with a plump berry, then dispose of the fruit. Before the sloe has shrivelled up, your wart will have vanished. Alternatively, rub the wart with a small piece of raw meat and hang the meat on a blackthorn spike for the same result. For magical workings, stab the point of a pen into a raw sloe to obtain the purple-black juice and write your charm on parchment, linen or cloth. Hang the charm on a blackthorn spike.

It is obvious that the folklore and superstitions surrounding the blackthorn are a result of thousands of years of cultural clashes and we would be well advised to strip away as much of the incoming, or non-native, beliefs as possible when exploring its power. Like most trees, it appears to have both benign and malevolent energies, depending on the period of history to which its folklore relates. Whatever we may feel about the tree, it really does herald the beginning of spring in a spectacular fashion.

---

### The Witch's Feast

*The killing of the family pig was an immensely important event for the future economy of the household. It was believed pigs that are killed between eight and ten of the clock in the morning will weigh more and be in better condition than they would be if killed at a layer time of day.* Although very few of us are reliant on home-cured meat this is an ideal opportunity to indulge ourselves whilst paying homage to the humble pig, who kept our ancestors alive during the long, cold winter months. What better way than by enjoying a bacon sandwich, or bacon and eggs for breakfast and placing a small offering outside for the local fauna!

---

# Chapter Fifteen

# November — Tree Moon

**November is the Tree Moon when trees felled earlier for winter fuel are replaced by new saplings – and represented by the Elder. This tree is considered unlucky by non-pagans but happens to be the tree of justice, since in times past judgements were often carried out beneath it. In some groups, the clan word of judgement is occasionally hafted with elder wood. The Anglo-Saxons referred to it as *Windmonath* (wind month) or *Blotmonath* (blood month) as this was the time to butcher livstock to lay down as salted meat for the winter. Traditionlly for people living closer to the land, it has marked a period of final preparation for the cold dark months ahead. In the 14th century misericord calendar, it was shown as the time for killing the pigs fattened with acorns during the previous month.**

This month marks *Samhain* and 'the month when all natural laws were suspended and the veil between the worlds was at its thinnest. Echoes of these ancient beliefs may still be sensed in the quiet depths of a damp, deserted lane, its death-like hush being broken only by the occasional sound of a startled bird.' (*Country Seasons*)

To the Celts it was the beginning of the New Year and *Samhain* (meaning 'end of summer') became the modern Irish Gaelic and Scottish Gaelic name for the month.

There is a bleakness about November that keeps people away from the woods and hedgerows, but for the witch who has the eyes to see, there is still beauty to be found in the frost laden spider's web, or the sprinkling of ice crystals on the old man's beard. Those dank, gloomy, foggy months of past memory are now extremely rare. Wintry sunshine has become much more common within the past 30 years but with it has come the increased rainfall turning farm tracks into glistening mud pools. This is the domain of the traditional witch …

### The Hag

*In a dirty hair lace*
*She leads on a brace*
*Of black-boar cats to attend her,*
*Who scratch at the moon,*
*And threaten at noon*
*Of night from heaven for to rend her.*

*A hunting she goes;*
*A cracked horn she blows,*
*At which the hounds fall a-bounding;*
*While the moon in her sphere*
*Peeps trembling for fear,*
*And night's afraid of the sounding.*

Handsome cock pheasants in all their glorious plumage are the main wild life feature this month. Pheasants seem to survive better than partridges during the winter months, probably because they are blessed with a formidable set of clawed feet, and their diet is more varied. Partridges, whose winter diet consists mainly of clover and grass, can find life particularly difficult if snow blankets the ground for any length of time. These little birds are easier to spot where cattle are being fed on silage or hay in cold weather as they share the feedstuffs.

One of the real signs of winter is the arrival of the first redwings that fly in from the Scandinavian winter. On first glance, it is easy to mistake this bird for a thrush except for the pale stripe above its eyes and a red patch by the flanks. Redwings are constantly on the move and will move around the country as the weather and food supplies dictate. They often fly by night, detected only by 'their chorus of thin, but far-carrying '*see-ip*' coming out of the darkness. Redwings are closely followed by the lapwings (or '*peewit*' from the cry) with their distinctive black and white plumage, feeding among the short green shoots of the winter wheat. Here there is plenty of bare earth where they can search for worms and insects. Their numbers are boosted by the arrival of the golden plovers with their speckled gold and brown winter plumage and cry of '*too-ee*'.

At dusk, one of the most spectacular sights is the daily gathering of starlings coming into roost. During the summer months, the ritual is carried out by males and non-breeding birds but in the winter the flight includes whole populations, often increased by the arrival of continental migrants. In both urban and rural locations, starlings gather to spend the night in communal roosts that may total some hundreds of thousands of birds.

Not all the birds fly in at once; they cover the skyscape in a swarming cloud, wheeling and diving in a fluid movement and is one of the most remarkable divinatory 'tools' at the witch's disposal. Known as a 'murmuration', these impressive flighting patterns can produce the most amazing images in the sky, which are held for a second and then disperse and regroup into something else. At dusk when the birds begin to gather over open fields, lean on your favourite gate and focus on the question you wish to ask. As with divination from clouds, this requires the witch to intuitively interpreting the aerial configurations to answer questions or predict a future outcome.

## The Hearth Fire

For those dark, cold November nights, when the witch has been out and about, there is nothing more welcoming than a hot, spicy supper. It is a perfect way of using leftover meat from the Sunday roast.

## Farmhouse Curry

*½ lb left-over lamb*
*1 tablespoon apple chutney*
*1 dessertspoon curry powder*
*2 tablespoons milk*
*1 tablespoon flour*
*1 apple*
*1 onion*
*2 oz butter*
*½ pint stock*

Chop meat finely. Melt the fat and when smoking hot fry the onion, flour, curry powder together for a few moments, stirring all the time. Add chopped apple, salt to taste, and stock. Stir constantly till sauce is smooth and boiling, then remove the pan to the side of the fire. Cover and simmer for 1/2 hour. Add the chopped meat. Thin to taste with a little milk. Stir in apple chutney and bring to the boil again. Add a few drops of lemon juice and milk. Serve at once on a hot dish with boiled rice.

The cleanly picked right shoulder blade of mutton was used for fortune telling in parts of Wales, right up to the turn of the 20th century, having been first mention by Gerald the Welshman (*Itinerary Through Wales*, 1188). The practice appears to have survived in the form of divination for identifying a future husband at All Hallows. The rhyme chanted as the blade bone was picked nine times was:

> *With this knife this bone I mean to pick:*
> *With this knife my lover's heart I mean to prick,*
> *Wishing him neither rest not sleep*
> *Until he comes to me to speak.*

Nine is a re-occurring magical number in Welsh folklore and the charm can obviously be adapted for all kinds of divination, since again love spells were the means of preserving other magical workings under the cover of country girls' games. Onions were also used for similar purposes. Up until 1900, girls in farming communities would name onions after bachelors in the area, which would then be stored in the loft. The first onion to sprout meant that the man would soon declare his love. If it didn't sprout he would remain a bachelor — or marry someone else. Indifferent lovers or husbands were tempted with 19th century love potions consisting of mead, cowslip or primrose wine put into a drinking horn, together with a cake made from small pieces of dough kept from nine bakings.

The wild foods available now are various forms of nut: beech, walnut, sweet chestnut and hazel nuts, and in times of hardship, roasted acorns have been used as a substitute for coffee. Pine kernels are the edible nuts of a certain variety of pine tree and are softer than most other nuts, with a delicate pine flavour. They may be eaten raw or added to salads, cooked vegetables and rice, or ground for sauces, such as *pesto*.

### Weatherwise

There are many regional variations on: *If the ice in November will bear a duck than all the rest will be slush and muck*, or *A cold November means a mild, wet winter* but this month offers a dark, dank landscape, often steeped in mist from morning till noon.

As Philip Clucas observes in *Country Seasons*, this is a season of 'bleakness that spreads Nature's dreary hue over the countryside', and a witch must now take delight in the simple things of the winter fields — the sprinkling of yellow blooms on the gorse, or the vivid scarlet of rose hips and holly.

### The Turning of the Year

In nature, November is the time of transition into winter, although autumn does not 'officially' end until late December in the astronomical divison of the seasons. The last leaves fall from the deciduous trees and many hibernating species commence their winter sleep.

**Then:** Pig killing.
**Now:** Beneath the fine tilth newly sown winter wheat.

**The Circle ritual for the month should be one of meditation and transition**. Perhaps a good idea is to reflect on the *faith* that is embodied in traditional witchcraft, and symbolised in the superstitions and folklore surrounding the forthcoming festivities and celebrations.

### Elder Magic

There are two 'goddess' trees that are found in the hedgerow. Hawthorn, sacred to the May Goddess, and Elder which belongs to the Crone and has so many virtues that, as we have seen, it is referred to as the 'poor man's medicine chest'. If there are any elder trees in your vicinity, you will soon gain one in your garden because birds drop the seeds after eating the fruit. The elder is a small tree or shrub that has a very mixed reputation in folklore. It features widely in Arthurian legends, Biblical tales and has always been associated with witchcraft and religion. In some parts of the country it is considered unlucky to take 'ellan-wood' into the house and to burn it would cause death within the family inside twelve months.

Elder also has a great number of folklore associations. It features in Arthurian tales and has long been associated with witchcraft and religion, which might explain why the Christians demonised it by having Judas hang himself from its branches and thereby making it a cursed tree! It has been suggested that the name elder derives from the Anglo-Saxon *eldrum*, meaning fire — but this is highly unlikely since elder does not burn very well and even most country people refused point-blank to burn it on the hearth fire.

In many areas of the country, there are tales of the Elder Mother or elder spirits who both inhabit the bush and who *are* the tree. Any cavalier treatment of the tree may result in all manner of calamities. It was believed that if a branch was cut and blood spurted from it, then likely as not the village witch was seen wearing a bandage or walking with a limp. If elder was taken into the house, death would be in the house within a year — put a baby in a cradle made of elder and the Faere Folk would steal it.

These beliefs make it necessary to take very special precautions should anyone wish to gather any wood for magical purposes. The elder should be approached with the head bare in the manner of a supplicant, with folded arms and partially bent legs — in a 'symbolic between the worlds pose with arms and legs neither bent nor straight'.

Let's make no bones about it, with the elder's reputation it is well to remember that you are approaching a very *real* magical and extremely powerful being. Tell the elder why you require its wood and what it will be used for. Wait for permission to be given and be prepared to give some recompense for what you take. A suitable invocation would be:

*Lady Ellhorn, give me some of thy wood.*
*And I will give thee some of mine*
*When it grows again in the forest.*

Wait for a moment of stillness to occur among the leaves and branches — this being the sign that the tree gives its permission. If there is a violent shaking of the leaves then permission has been denied and you should not proceed. Whatever you cut should then be taken 'wrong handed'. There are numerous modern tales of the bad luck or illness suffered by those who ignored this warning — and equally good fortune coming the way of those who show the right amount of reverence.

Despite all its beneficial uses, elder wood should never be burnt on a domestic fire and there is a definite ban on including it on the Beltaine fire because of its associations with the Faere Folk, even though it is one of the Nine Sacred Woods. Be warned: One witch tried to break the ellen-wood's curse by arranging for a landscape gardener to cut down the tree. Family fortunes took an immediate nose-dive and it took years for both the tree and the family to recover. If you have an elder growing in the garden, let it thrive and see how your fortune changes — just have a little word whenever it needs pruning!

The name of the Elder Mother in the supplication reveals the elder's connection with the Faere Folk and musical instruments as *ellhorn* literally means 'elf horn' i.e. pipes which suggests that the Little People used its wood for that purpose. Magically the wood is used in personal charms to turn aside curses and banish malevolent spirits from the vicinity. These charms can be placed around the inside of the home for the same purpose. Elder leaves gathered at Beltaine are especially powerful and bunches hung over the doors and windows prevent any negative forces entering. The leaves can also be dried and added to protective pouches although some people find the smell of elder offensive.

The elder has, of course, plenty of Otherworld associations. It is the gateway between the worlds — whether the kingdom of the dead or the lands of the Faere Folk — the Elder Mother acts as the gatekeeper. This is why it was believed that sleeping beneath the tree could enable you to make contact with the Mighty Dead; this was also a risky business as it was said that there was the risk of not waking up again!

Rather than run this risk but still be able to utilise the elder's powers when astral journeying, hang a bunch of leaves above the bed and take an infusion of the flowers or berries, — or better still, a glass of elderberry wine.

## The Witch's Yuletide Divination

*If a sprig of holly is thrown on the fire and burns with a crackling noise, it is a sign that the auspices will be fine; but if it burns with a dull flame and does not crackle, it is a sign that all will not be well in the coming year.* Divination by flames to foretell the future is thought to be one of the first methods ever used. The intensity of the flames, as well as the shape and form they take, is considered when diving the future or interpreting omens.

Chapter Seventeen

# December — Long Night Moon

**Yule time and the Long Night Moon is represented by the Holly, symbol of the winter aspect of the god as the Holly King and sacred to the Horned God; it has been used as a decoration at the Midwinter festival for centuries and was used for the same purpose at the Roman *Saturnalia*. The Anglo-Saxon called it *Wintermonath*. Other ancient names refer to the Norse winter festival of Yule, or to the darkness of the period (as in the modern Scottish-Gaelic name *Dubhlachd*). In the 14th century misericord calendar, it was shown as the time for spinning by the fire. Winter Solstice falls on or around 21st**

On patches of bare ground and along the edges of fields where the grass is short, evidence can be found of rabbit scrapes. These small, horseshoe-shaped holes are an inch or more deep and show where the rabbits have been digging for succulent roots as part of their winter diet. This is the time of short days and long, dark nights although we can be sure to witness some spectacular sunrises and sunsets as the rays tinge the frosty landscape a delicate pink. The low sun casts squat shadows along the hedgerow, while deep in the woods there is a frozen stillness, except for the rooks circling noisily overhead. In the stillness of the frozen morning, high overhead a robin thrills out its melodious song.

In the depths of winter, often the only greenery to be seen is that of the ivy, clinging to trees, old walls and farm buildings, providing shelter for hibernating insects. Among the flowering disks, the insects can feed on the rich supplies of nectar, which is a rare thing at this desolate time of the year. According to one source, this sweet liquid can be so intoxicating that if the ivy is shaken, drunken insects will fall to the ground. Through January and February, the small green berries will mature, ripening into black fruits in the spring. As a result of all this insect activity, in mid-winter you will see a wide variety of birds poking around amongst the leaves.

In winter and spring, a flock of pigeons can decimate a field of sprouting crops. A single pigeon eats a large handful of grain or seedlings a day, so a flock of 1,000 birds can strip acres of arable land in a day. The pigeon's swirling flight makes it an awkward target and illustrates why true sporting guns prefer to test their skill with this bird rather than the cumbersome pheasant. They are deceptively fast and if you show yourself too early, they turn and swing away and if you leave it too late, they are gone and you are left shooting into thin air. Its rural name is the 'ringed dove', which refers to the distinctive white markings on the neck and wings. The soft *coo* of the wood pigeon has a soothing and sleepy sound during spring and summer days, but it belies the damage these birds can cause to crops. There is an old Wessex rhyme:

*Sow four beans as you make your row,*
*One for to rot and one to grow,*
*And one for the pigeon and one for the crow.*

The bird is a late nester and produces two broods just as the harvest is ripening. The young chicks are known as squabs and are fed on 'pigeon milk', a cheesy-like substance rich in protein, which the parents regurgitate from the crop. It is the only bird to produce milk similar to that of mammals. Pigeons are best eaten young but older birds can be used in casseroles and stews.

## Wood pigeon with gravy and peas

*4x8oz wood pigeons*

*salt and pepper*
*2 tblsp vegetable oil*
*1 celery stalk, chopped*
*1 onion, peeled and chopped*
*1 carrot, peeled and chopped*
*2 cloves garlic, peeled and halved*
*4 fl ozs white wine*
*sprig of thyme and a bay leaf*
*8 fl ozs chicken stock*
*7 oz streaky bacon*
*1¾ lb fresh (or frozen) peas*
*1 fl ozs pigeon gravy*

Heat the oven to 400F/200C/Gas Mk 6. Season the pigeon and seal on both sides in 1 tablespoon of oil. Place in the heated oven and cook for 12 minutes. Allow to rest for five minutes. Place the celery, onion, carrot and garlic in the tray the pigeon was cooked in and roast to a golden colour. Add the white wine, thyme and bay leaf and a little salt and pepper. Boil and reduce until the liquid has virtually evaporated. Add the stock plus any juices from the rested pigeon. Bring to the boil and simmer for 3 minutes. Pass through a sieve and into a sauceboat. Cut the bacon into thin strips and fry in the remaining oil. Blanch the peas in salted water for 3 minutes and drain. Add the pigeon gravy and peas to the bacon and reduce until it has nearly evaporated. Season with salt and pepper.

or

## Pigeon Casserole

*2 oz butter*
*3 slices lean bacon, chopped*
*8 spring onions, trimmed and chopped*
*8 oz button mushrooms, wiped clean and halved*

*breasts from four pigeons*
*1 pint water*
*4 teaspoons tomato purée*
*grated rind of lemon.*

In a large frying pan, melt the butter and when the foam subsides add the bacon and spring onions and cook until the bacon is lightly browned. Remove from the pan and place in a large ovenproof casserole. Place the pigeon breasts in the frying pan and cook them, turning frequently until they are lightly browned. Transfer to the casserole. Add the mushrooms to the pan and cook for about 3 mins or until they are well coated with butter. Tip the contents of the pan over the meat. Return the pan to the heat, pour in the water and stir in the tomato purée and lemon rind. When the liquid boils, remove the pan from the heat and pour contents into the casserole. Cover and place in the oven for 1 hour or until the breasts are tender when pierced with the point of a sharp knife. (350F, 180C, Mark 4) Remove casserole from the oven and serve immediately with mashed potatoes and steamed French beans.

The seasonal growth of mistletoe is an old gipsy cure for epilepsy and is listed as such in *Flora Britannica*. There are many tales of the gipsy woman telling the parents of a severely epileptic child to 'boil some mistletoe and give the child a wineglass of the water to drink'. The child's father tried it himself and having suffered no side effects, did as she said and the child never had another attack.

Although associated with the Druids and their sacred oaks, this parasitic plant is rarely found on oak trees. It commonly grows on poplar, apple, lime and hawthorn but oak-mistletoe is so unusual that the Druids would have attached special significance to it. Squash a couple of Yuletide berries against the bark of a suitable tree and watch the emerging seedlings take root.

In Glamorgan and Monmouthshire, the Midwinter celebrations were embellished by the *Mari Lwyd*, although in other parts of Wales the ceremony was associated with the New Year and Twelfth Night. Whenever the *Mari Lwyd* was observed, it was carried over several days. Like many folk customs, the origins are obscure but it is believed to be connected with Celtic horse-worship, since the name means 'grey Mary' or 'grey mare', and the celebrants carry around a horse's skull on a pole with a white sheet draped over it. The party consisted of 'impromptu poets and singers who challenged those inside to a rhyming contest' and the householders could keep them out so long as they could answer the rhyme. Failure to do so entitled the supporters of *Mari Lwyd* to food and drink on the house.

## The Hearth Fire

In the witch's kitchen, the pantry should be stocked with all kinds of pickles and preserves made during the autumn. This is the time for entertaining family and friends and creating a homely atmosphere of warmth and hospitality. As we observed earlier, if we want to, we can stretch the celebrations from the old Roman festival of Saturnalia on the 17th December until Twelfth Night on the 6th January when old Yule coincides with the Julian calendar.

The witch will have made her own provisions for the coming Midwinter celebration to welcome back the Sun-King and among these should be an ash-faggott, made up of ash twigs, to be burned to ensure good fortune. A miniature one can be kept in the house for good luck. Everyone's attention will be on the coming festivities, just as they have been for thousands of years — as people waited for the 'longest night' to herald the approaching spring. Next to the Harvest Home, perhaps the Midwinter Festival is the second most important festival in the calendar of the traditional witch.

## Suggestions for a Traditional Midwinter Feast

### First Course
Scotch broth, potato or artichoke soup,
or hors d'oeuvres with sardines, liver sausage, potato salad and
beetroot flavoured with your own dried herbs

### Second Course
Roast goose or 'cottage goose' (rolled, stuffed pork),
or roast pheasant

### Accompaniments
Baked potatoes, buttered peas and Brussels sprouts.
Serve your homemade preserves with pork or goose,
and small bacon-wrapped sausages with any bird.

### Third Course
Plum pudding and custard sauce, flavoured with rum or
brandy, or mince pies with brandy butter and sloe gin.

### Dessert
Oranges, bananas, dates, figs and nuts.

With wild boar back in fashion, it can make a welcome change
from that American import — the turkey. Wild boar was used for
more than a 1,000 years to mark the festive season in this country
and the boar's head with an apple in its mouth, dates back to the
Norse Yule pig sacrifice at the turn of the year. The boar was
sacred to both the Celt and the Norse people, who believed that
its flesh was the food of the heroes of Valhalla.

The ceremony of the Boar's Head is still observed in Queen's
College, Oxford, as it has been since 1341, on the last Saturday
before Christmas. The head decorated with sprigs of rosemary,
holly and bay, with an orange in its mouth is presented to the

Provost and Fellows at the High Table, while the choir sings *The Boar's Head Carol*:

> *The bores hed in handis I brynge*
> *With garlands gay and birdis syngynge*
> *I pray you all helpe me to synge*
> *Que estis inconvinio.*

And for those who over-indulge, there is the traditional pick-me-up that is also a comfort drink given to invalids — the posset.

## A Soothing Yule Posset

*1 pint milk*
*6 fl ozs white wine*
*2 oz brown sugar*
*1 lemon*
*1 teaspoon ground or fresh ginger*
*Grating of nutmeg*

Boil the milk, pour in the wine and let the mixture cool until it curdles. Strain off the curds, add the sugar, the whole lemon and spices. Serve like yoghurt.

Even though Nature has battened down the hatches until spring, the greyness of the landscape is broken by a flash of scarlet from the hips on the wild briar. Even at this dead time, there is still a harvest to be taken in and used as a valuable dose of Vitamin C during the winter months to follow. The wild briar rose with its delicate shell pink colouring is a common sight during the summer months. In autumn the roses give way to scarlet berries known as hips that become fully ripe in December; these were eaten as 'winter fruits' in Anglo-Saxon times when the pureed fruit, deseeded and mixed with wine and sugar, was served as a dessert. Hips were made into syrup that could be added to cough mixture and jam.

## Rosehip Syrup

For rosehip syrup, you'll need about 2 lb of ripe fruit and 1 lb of sugar. Cover the hips with water, boil for ten minutes, mash and strain. Add the sugar, boil again for five minutes and bottle. Including the same amount of apples produces a pleasant 'honey'. A 16th century recipe adds sugar, cinnamon, ginger and lemon juice to the stewed fruit to make a puree for tarts and toppings. Make sure you extract all the prickly seeds, as these can be a dangerous internal irritant.

## Weatherwise

The traditional December weather as depicted in paintings and Victorian pictures, with frozen ponds and deep snow, is no longer an annual occurance in much of Britain. Although there are still sharp frosts to trim the branches, hedges and rooftops with white crystal that gleam in the morning sunlight. On 31st December, however, attention turns to the direction of the wind:

*If New Year's Eve night the wind blow south,*
*It betokeneth warmth and growth;*
*Iof west, much milk and fish in the sea;*
*If north, much cold and storms there will be;*
*If east, the trees will bear much fruit;*
*If north-east, flee it, man and brute.*

## The Turning of the Year

December is the dead, naked month of long nights, brief days and a countryside shrouded in grey mist. 'Within the emptiness of barren fields, crows glide like shadowed ghouls, emitting heavy cries that seem to match the month's drear atmosphere', observes Philip Clucos in *Country Seasons*.

**Then:** Spinning by the fire.
**Now:** In the damp and cold fields, new wheat emerges.

The Circle ritual for this month should acknowledge that from this yearly death, a new countryside will emerge, *vital and lush with springtime's fertile breath.* The Yule log symbolises the idea of this rebirth of light, i.e. the Sun. The Midwinter festival is the start of longer, lighter days as the Lord of the Sun arises from the Lady of the Land.

## Holly Magic

The oak-log symbolises the regeneration of the earth at Winter Solstice but at this time of the year, the attention is on the holly and between the beginning of the month and the Winter Solstice (21st) the scarlet berries on the holly will become more and more spectacular. The kind of holly brought into a couple's home for their first Midwinter Festival together is of great significance. If the holly leaves have sharp prickles (known as he-holly) the man will be master of the marriage; if the holly has no prickles, or the prickles feel soft and flexible (she-holly) then the woman will rule the marriage. Some folklore says this only holds true for one year, so the same procedure needs to be carried out at each Midwinter Festival to find the dominant partner for the following twelve-month.

The wood of the holly gives a hot fire, but burns very quickly but the wood can be burned 'green' (freshly cut) without waiting for it to dry. Magically, a witch would use holly to keep intruders at bay and return spells to their sender, so use holly in charm bags and incense for all defensive rituals; in times of greatest danger position sprigs of holly around the boundary of your home to keep out all negative forces. When out walking at night, a holly cane or staff will keep you safe from all mischievous entities — at one time, no coachman would drive at night unless the handle of his whip was fashioned from holly wood. A wand made of holly is also very useful in keeping unruly spirits under control.

Holly also works well as a guardian of domestic animals.

Fasten a little to any animal's collar to keep it safe when away from your protective influence, and be sure to hang a sprig in any outbuildings where animals are kept, both to make them thrive and to protect them from the attentions of the Faere Folk. In country lore, it is said that if you throw a spring of holly after a runaway animal, it will return of its own accord.

*The Holly and the ivy*
*When they are both full grown*
*Of all the tree in the Green Wood*
*The holly bears the crown ...*

---

### A Witch's First Footing

Although First Footing is regarded as the archetypal Scottish custom, it was previously common in England and Wales.

**People are very particular as to whether they see a man or woman the first thing on New Year's morning in order to secure good luck for the coming year. As a rule the majority deem it lucky to see a man, but unlucky to see a woman ... if he be fair, especially red-haired he brings luck; if he be dark-haired he in unlucky.**

When observing the custom, remember it is very important that the 'first footer' should bring some gift, as if he (or she) comes empty-handed, misfortune will follow.

---

Chapter Seventeen

# December/January — Ice Moon and the Sacred Space

December/January is the time of the Ice Moon which only occurs every three years as the moon's progression changes — represented by the Yew as a symbol of mystical journeying between the worlds. This is the tree of death and resurrection and some of the oldest yews are to be found in churchyards. It is a very long-lived tree and its evergreen foliage is regarded as symbol of immortality.

As we've seen, for the witch an old hedge is the bond with a landscape our ancestors had known. Its stile marks the ancient right of way that for centuries led from the edge of the parish to the church green; the old hedge reflecting the changing life of the local villages, and the world beyond. After a thousand years, however, the hedgerow's gifts of fuel and food are now largely ignored or unrecognised. Some witches continue to take its fruits to make jam, jellies and wine, but few claim its small wood for kindling the hearth fire — and fewer still know the secrets of its medicine chest and magical properties.

## Yew Magic

The yew is an evergreen tree that is extremely long lived, making it the perfect symbol of immortality. Old yew trees are often found in churchyards and may be much older than the church buildings — and so show evidence of being old pagan sites. This tree is a protector of Otherworld and the spirits of the dead; through the yew ancestral spirits can be contacted. And as witches of traditional Craft, we must also face the fact that if we acknowledge and accept the 'Ol Lad as the Sacrificial King and protector, we must also pay homage to him as the Hunter and bringer of death.

## The Sacred Space

In magical working, the Circle protects from any negative or hostile intrusion by creating a barrier between this world and Otherworld. It also acts as a 'holding tank' for the magical energy raised during the Circle working, which is to be harnessed and directed at the matter in hand. If it were not for the Circle, the energy would flow off in all directions and dissipate; the Circle keeps it confined to a small area and concentrates it. To all intent and purpose, when setting up the Circle we are preparing a sacred space, which requires ritual purification and consecration if the spell is to work properly.

In *Traditional Witchcraft for Field and Hedgerow,* however, the casting of a Circle in the open landscape is to bar entry to the very natural energies we wish to absorb. The answer is that we must find our own natural sacred space that we can cleanse and prepare for magical working. **Remember, nothing in Nature is profane ... only human influence can cause a place to become 'unclean'.**

Initially we may not be aware that a hidden corner may become our own personal — and secret — sacred place. During the year, however, there will be one spot to which we return again and again. It is a place where we can remain unseen but even if we are noticed, there is nothing about our actions to incite a casual observer's interest. It may be one of the places where we stop in our meanderings and pause for a while ...

- **a small sandy beach by a river or stream**. This may be overhung with hawthorn; concealed by the buttress of a bridge ... or actually under the bridge itself.
- **a wooded corner of field.** A place where young trees and

bracken conceal the place from prying eyes and the only other domestic visitors are sheep.

- **a double hedge**. A truly magical place where boundaries meet and twin hedges have grown up from the original earthen boundary markers.
- **a patch of clear ground beneath an old tree**. A sloping bank beneath an old oak or beech tree that provides a comfortable place to sit and watch the world go by.
- **a moss-covered boulder or boundary stone**. Many of these large stones were deposited by melting glaciers and can be found all over the landscape in the most unlikely places.
- **an isolated group of trees**. Or even a single tree in the middle of a park or field.

... in fact, it can be anywhere where we feel comfortable and at peace. At some stage during a year of walking the fields, lanes and hedgerows, this place will reveal itself as being somewhere special — somewhere *magical*. This is where we come to recharge our batteries; to think or meditate; to unwind and relax. This is our own personal point of contact for drawing on natural energy that will enhance us magically when we introduce them into our Circle workings.

Once we have identified this special place, we need to prepare it for use as a channel of natural energy. Make a switch from broom, hazel or birch twigs and clear away all the dead leaves and twigs, brushing until bare earth, moss or grass is revealed. There only needs to be a magical cleansing if there is evidence of human contamination. If this is the case, seriously consider finding another space or, ritually cleanse the whole area with consecrated water taken from a local stream or spring, and mixed with salt. Liberally sprinkle the consecrated water all over the sacred space, using the repeated chant: *Begone, foul and pestilent congregation!*

**Warning:** Always check when re-visiting the place that there has been no repeated human has defilement before attempting to channel any natural energy, or your subsequent magical workings will be corrupted.

As we learned at the beginning, no book ever written can teach us how to become a witch. Only Nature can do that. Only Nature can coax out those long suppressed abilities and give us back the freedom to be a traditional witch. Throughout the days, weeks and months of the year, we observe and register the subtle changes on 'our patch' until it becomes second nature. Our totem animals bring signs from Otherworld pertaining to future events or omens.

As we tramp the damp fields, shady lanes and tangled hedgerows, we will collect a variety of bits and pieces that will be of magical use to us in the privacy of our indoor Circle workings. Whether we use the traditional nine-foot Circle, or encase ourselves inside an electric blue sphere, the objects we bring from the countryside become part of our magical equipment for that particular working. These 'power' objects require no ritual cleansing or we will lose the essence of the very thing we are using to generate natural energy.

Once the Circle is cast, we begin by visualising our sacred space and imagine ourselves seated there, breathing in the familiar smells and atmosphere generated by that particular place. Depending on the nature of our Circle working, we will also have corresponding flora or piece from an appropriate tree to aid visualisation. If we are engaged in astral journeying, for example, then a feather or tuft of fur from our totem fauna will provide the link necessary to guide us on our way. To dispose of the object once the Circle working is over, either burn it, cast it into fast running water, or bury it in your favourite hedgebank.

Unfortunely, no longer maintained in the traditional style — kept close and low — the hedgerow develops a ragged silhouette, even becoming an obstacle for modern farming techniques. As we watch these hedgrows disappear, traditional witches must have their misgivings ... The soil will be eroded and the birds that kept th pasture clean will leave ... there will be a plague of insects. A witch quickly learns to recognise where the natural balance has been tilted – and she knows there is always a price to pay. **So let's walk through the fields and along the hedgerow together and discover Nature as she moves through the year ... before it's too late.**

# Bibliography & Sources

*Ancient Trees: Living Landscapes,* Richard Muir (Tempus)

*Book of the British Countryside,* AA (Drive Publications)

*The Book of Divining the Future,* Eva Shaw (Wordsworth)

*The Cloudspotter's Guide,* Gaven Pretor-Pinney (Daily Telegraph Books)

*The Country Book of the Year,* Dennis L Furnell (David & Charles)

*The Covenant of the Wild,* Stephen Budiansky (Phoenix)

*The Encyclopaedia of Herbs and their uses,* Deni Brown (D&K)

*Fauna Britannica,* Stefan Buczacki (Hamlyn)

*Flora Britannica,* Richard Mabey (Random House)

*Folklore, Myths & Customs of Britain,* Marc Alexander (Sutton)

*Food For Free,* Richard Mabey (Collins)

*Green Pharmacy,* Barbara Griggs (Norman & Hobhouse)

*Hedgerow,* Eric Thomas & John T White (Dorling Kindersley)

*The History of Food,* Maguelonne Toussaint-Samat (Wiley-Blackwell)

*Memory, Wisdom & Healing: The History of Domestic Plant Medicine,* Gabrielle Hatfield (Sutton)

*The Penguin Guide to the Superstitions of Britain and Ireland,* Steve Roud (Penguin)

*Root & Branch: British Magical Tree Lore,* Draco & Harriss (ignotus)

*Wild Food,* Roger Phillips (Pan)

*The Witch's Treasury of the Countryside,* Draco & Harriss (ignotus)

*A Year in the Life of a Field,* Michael Allaby (David & Charles)

Moon Books invites you to begin or deepen your
encounter with Paganism, in all its rich, creative,
flourishing forms